ENDORSEMENTS FOR
BREATHE AGAIN

If ever a book was sent by God to a particular 'time and people', it is this book – for this is the time, and we are those people. *Breathe Again* came to me during a season of personal exhaustion, and dare I say, burn out. With fresh revelation and simple clarity, the words became much-needed sips of water to my thirsty soul. I encourage you to drink deeply of these truths, and find your way back to Eden . . . the place we were created to live.

Karen Wheaton
Founder and Leader of The Ramp

Every hour, my Apple Watch pings to remind me to breathe. This always strikes me as quite funny: I was born breathing and I've been doing just fine ever since, so why do I need to be told to do what I already do? Maybe it's because I take breathing for granted. Maybe it's reminding me how important it is to breathe and why I should pause and take deep breaths. Andy's new book, *Breathe Again*, is doing the same thing. Andy Elmes is a student of the God-breathed Word. He is also an outstanding writer who brings his research and ideas to life in a way that resonate for the reader. Just as with his other books, Andy communicates life-giving truths. I have read all of Andy's books, and each time I am inspired and motivated. Not surprisingly, after reading *Breathe Again*, I am profoundly stirred. I highly applaud this book!

Dr. Leon van Rooyen
President of Global Theological University

I have worked closely with Andy and Gina Elmes since they planted Family Church in 1997. It's a true honour to serve God with someone who really lives out what he preaches and sustains an unwavering depth of relationship with God through the difficult times as well as the good. Andy has discovered the joy of being a 'branch' that abides in the Vine, drawing daily on the life of God's Spirit in order to bear much fruit. Our church was founded on this truth and Andy has made it his mission to bring God's people into a revelation of this truth, hence this book. Whether you've just come to faith in Jesus or you've been walking with the Lord for years, this book will help you to cease striving and walk in all that God has given you by His amazing grace.

Steuart Payne
Executive Pastor, Family Church UK

In *Breathe Again*, Pastor Andy Elmes rewires your thinking. He reintroduces you to the Gospel that rescues man from the exhaustion of "mere existence" and brings him into the abundance of God's rest. However, this book is not about relaxation and comfort. It's about the fullness of life God always intend and has now restored. You will learn foundational truths that create a sustainable rest in your life, and in the last chapter, Pastor Andy puts the icing on the cake by equipping you with practical action steps. Make sure you read this all the way to the end! Furthermore, this book is effective not only because of the words on the page, but also because of the life from which the words flow. Pastor Andy's friendship and ministry has personally refreshed me again and again. One of the first times I met Pastor Andy, he spoke these words over me: "You are at your best when you are at rest." Those words have become a guiding principle in my life that daily brings me into the ease of God's grace. I encourage you to open your heart as I have and allow Pastor Andy's ministry to refresh you, challenge you, and renew you by the power of the Holy Spirit.

Micah Wood
Head of Ramp School of Ministry

Breathe Again

Breathe Again

HOW TO EXPERIENCE THE LIFE OF GOD HERE ON EARTH

Andy Elmes

DEDICATION

Dedicated to my Dad, Dave Elmes.

Thank you for being such a great dad. You brought me into this life naturally but you and Mum also led me to Jesus and helped me to find the brand new life He would give me. I want to honour you for the example you have been to me throughout the years of faithfulness, loyalty and courage. From the early days of selling fruit and vegetables together to now extending the kingdom of God together you have always been there with your support and love. Thank you.

Love you, Dad.

Andy

ACKNOWLEDGEMENTS

I'd like to acknowledge the support of a few people whose input into my life, and the writing of this book, has been invaluable.

GINA

Thank you once again for putting up with my quirky ways as I spent hours walking, praying and lost in my computer typing. Your love and support constantly makes me strong and enables me to concentrate on and fulfil all the things the Lord asks us to do. I love you more than words could ever say and thank God for you always. Thank you.

PASTOR COLIN URQUHART

You have become a dear friend, and a valued and trusted voice in my life. Our times of meeting up to talk and pray have become precious moments in my month. Your input into my life has been profound and always leaves me feeling closer to God, and that the things He is asking of me are more than possible. You are a true legend, Sir – what you have seen and experienced in God over many years of faithful ministry needs to be heard by many in our nation. I am so, so thankful for the time you have given me to know you more and sit under your ministry.

MY PASTORS

Thank you for always giving me the space to pursue God and for always encouraging me to run faster after Him. The way you all run with the things He places on my heart is a continued blessing to my life and I thank Him for you and your families often. Together we are truly making a difference and the best is yet to come.

MATT LOCKWOOD

Thanks, Matt, you did it again – helping me to take the messages and thoughts God placed on my heart and turn them into a book for others to experience and enjoy. Thank you for your patience, experience and faithfulness. You help to make writing a book very easy.

CONTENTS

FOREWORD

I was awakened this morning by a blessed bombardment of words regarding the breath of God, with an urge to return to Genesis chapter one. This first chapter of the Bible has lately become freshly alive as I have begun to see it as seminal – that is, significant as a resource. The thought that sealed the matter of bounding out of bed to set down these words was 'He's still at it!'

What started in Genesis is still going on! God's creative activity continues unabated. What He began, He blessedly continues in the present time. He is still the 'I am', the One who was, is and will be. He has never ceased being God, nor has He ceased His work as God. It is of note that the name of God in this creation story is *Elohim*, a name for God that is used over two thousand, seven hundred times in the Old Testament and, significantly, thirty-two times in the first chapter of Genesis alone. This name is of great and intriguing significance in so many ways, not least of which is that it is first used in the Creation story, is intensively plural, and declares the multiplicity and continuity of our Creative God.

And that is what I hear crying out throughout the entirety of this message by my friend Andy Elmes. Here is what I hear Andy saying: 'God did all this, yes! But this God is still at work. Whatever He has done, He is still doing. Whatever He has seen, He is still seeing. Whatever He has said, He is still saying.'

Breathing is related to life as well as speech. Where there is no breath, there is neither life nor speech. Unfortunately, it is debated in our world today whether or not God still speaks. I call this the 'hovering heresy', which basically declares that God once spoke, then produced a book and promptly fell silent, totally mute. We are correct to love our Bible, revere it and read it, but we must never jettison the over-arching thought that this God of Genesis is still active in our world today, still breathing, still speaking, still acting and living in each of us by the Spirit of Jesus.

Andy has been conquered by this here-and-now God, the Eternal I am, who was and is and is to come. This book exudes with the life and breath of God, and challenges us to adore the past, anticipate the future and dare to live in the moment. If this God is eternal – and He is – His past can be proved, His future guaranteed and His continuing presence can be presently enjoyed as well as be empowering.

Thanks, Andy Elmes, for repeated reminders, forcefully and clearly presented, that let us know GOD'S STILL AT IT!

Jack R. Taylor, President
Dimensions Ministries, Melbourne, Florida, USA

INTRODUCTION

*D*o you sometimes feel almost breathless, struggling to keep up with the pace of life even in your Christianity? Does it feel like you are constantly living on the edge of the page without any real margins in your life? That instead of breathing the nice, deep breaths of life that God has designed for you, you are almost hyperventilating as you try to keep up with the demands of life? Or maybe you just have a sense that there must be a better way of breathing than that which you have known up to now.

If so then I believe this book is going to indeed be a 'breath of fresh air' in your life, putting to an end the overwhelming sense of mere existence you've been living with until now. In some ways it will be very much like a spiritual massage – by that I mean it has been written with the purpose of releasing a fresh burst of God's life in you. Sometimes the text may seem repetitive concerning certain truths we stay focused on and return to, but this is actually deliberate and intentional because, as with a natural, deep-tissue massage, I want to work repetitively in the same area of some of the things we have believed with the purpose of releasing fresh, spiritually-oxygenated blood into them. Just as a natural massage releases you from knots in your body that cause discomfort or a lesser experience of living so, using God's Word, I am about to massage some spiritual knots in your life to see freshness and freedom run through them, bringing greater health, life and well-being.

The content and theme of this book flows out of a personal revelation I had in which I felt the Lord bring me out of striving and into His rest. Understanding that His breath – His life – is now available to us is a life-changing thing, but knowing how to experience it is vital. In this book we are going to visit verses that reveal in glorious Technicolor the life that God intended for us to know and then show the simple pathway back into the fullness of it. Written in a progressive way, each chapter naturally leads into, and builds upon, the one before – just like massage – constantly increasing the depth of our understanding to remove every knot so you can experience His life in abundance.

Over the course of the book we will visit some well-known truths as well as some lesser-known ones. We will add a fuller context to things we have partially understood with a heart to come into the fullness of truth concerning what the Lord has made available for us to know as His new, fully-redeemed creations.

So are you ready to discover how He made you to breathe, to come into His rest and discover a carefree life? Then let's get this journey started. I pray this book ministers to and refreshes your life – spirit, soul and body.

Andy

But because of his great love for us, God, who is rich in mercy, made us alive with Christ even when we were dead in transgressions—it is by grace you have been saved. And God raised us up with Christ and seated us with him in the heavenly realms in Christ Jesus.

EPHESIANS 2:4-6 (NIV)

And you, being dead in your trespasses and the uncircumcision of your flesh, He has made alive together with Him, having forgiven you all trespasses.

COLOSSIANS 2:13 (NKJV)

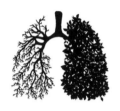

Chapter 1

SETTING THE SCENE

"Am I breathing like God designed me to?"

'That is a very good question,' I remember thinking to myself, when the Lord first dropped it into my heart! It was during the summer of 2018, and I had taken my wife Gina and our kids to America for an extended break. It was a season of life where we were celebrating some important anniversaries and birthdays that were all around the same time: Gina and I had been married twenty-five years, our eldest daughter was turning twenty-one, my son was turning eighteen and another daughter was becoming a teenager. We thought that we should mark this special season with a big family road trip around the United States. We carefully planned a trip that would take a month and would enable us to see some different parts of America that we had not seen or spent much time in before. Prior to leaving I told the key leaders of our church, Family Church, about how I was going to use this time to press deeper into God and find out what His strategies were for what He had in store for us next. In my mind I was going to get refreshed – of course I was – but more importantly I was going to get re-envisioned and fired up for our next season in ministry. That was my plan anyway. Little did I know that the Lord had another plan which could not have been more opposite.

So we landed in New York City and immediately made our way upstate. If you have ever been to Upstate

New York then you'll know that it is completely different to New York City. Instead of buildings and concrete there are mountains, forests and lakes. We were staying near the beautiful Catskill Mountains. Here, deer run around wild like cats do in the UK, and all manner of wildlife can wander through your garden each and every day. Some dear friends of ours, Jaron and Brenda, surprised us with a cabin they had booked for us. It was located in the woods and was beautifully rustic, but with all the modern comforts city dwellers like us think they need. There were no other houses nearby. In every direction all you could see were trees filled with squirrels, and all you could hear was the sound of birds singing and the scurrying of chipmunks in the surrounding bushes. This place was certainly very different from my normal city life back home, where the usual sound that fills my back garden is that of arguing neighbours or the speeding traffic on the busy motorway, which is only a stone's throw away.

We got to the cabin fairly late on that first night and we all went straight to bed – we were very tired from travelling and we were all ready for a good night's rest. Very early the next morning I was awoken by the dawn chorus, and jumped straight out of bed with the intention of getting straight down to 'doing business' with the Lord. I knew that there was no rush and although I had a month to do this, I did not want to waste a single minute of my time away. I went out to sit on the rustic wooden front porch with a freshly brewed cup of coffee in one hand and my Bible and journal in the other – I was ready for some serious Kingdom business. With my pen poised, I looked around once again at the beautiful surroundings and I began to pray prayers such as: 'Okay, Lord, what have you got to teach me?', 'Okay, Lord, let's do business', 'So, Lord, what do you want to deal with in my life and what are the battle plans for seeing an awakening in the UK?'

I had prayed like this at other times when I had gone away and it always seemed to work, but this time was different. Every time I prayed or started to meditate on God and His Word, all I would get in response were two very simple words. A little annoyed, I continued to shut out everything that I thought could be a distraction and I repented of anything that may have been 'blocking my breakthrough'. In fact, I tried everything I knew to do but all I kept getting were the same two very simple words. No matter how hard I strived it felt as though the Lord was saying, 'I am not playing, Andy. You are on your own.' Over and over again they came, the same two little words, but later on I would discover that those two words were everything I actually needed – I just didn't realise it straight away. So what were those two words, I hear you ask? What were these two words that would completely reshape the landscape of my life and everything that I was doing? Two words that would set a brand-new, more enjoyable and sustainable pace for my life. They were two very simple words that contained a powerful supernatural breakthrough. 'Tell us what they were!', I hear you cry. Okay, they were: *restore* and *breathe*. That's it! Every time I prayed or tried to press in to hear something else from the Lord, all I would hear was either: 'restore' or 'breathe'.

Restore? I thought I was certain that I did not need restoration. I needed strategy. I needed God to supercharge me for whatever was next. Looking back I can see that God's plan was to restore me in order to supercharge me. As I sat and thought about this word 'restore', the Holy Spirit began to bring a freshness into my understanding of Father God as a redemptive restorer. He does not just restore the physical or seen things in our lives but He also restores the internal, unseen things. Just as it says so poetically in Psalm 23:2-3:

He leads us by still waters, causes us to lay down in green pastures and restoreth our souls.

It soon became obvious to me that God's agenda for that month was to restore my soul by bringing it fresh life, health and well-being. That was His plan for the month, even though it was not mine. Did I feel broken, weary or deflated? No, that was the strange thing. I did not feel that way at all. Everything in my life seemed to be going well, despite a few challenges. But even they were progressing forward in a healthy way. We were actually experiencing some real miracles in our lives; it was a good season in the ministry. From my perspective I did not think I needed a time of restoration at all, but perspective is a very interesting thing, isn't it? It's amazing how we can get used to such a fast pace for our lives that we can no longer correctly see when we actually need to take time out.

We can be living so fast that we don't always allow the Restorer to bring His restoration to the inner, unseen parts of what makes us who we are as we should? Yet, in His Fatherly loving kindness God will sometimes put the brakes on the pace we are running at because He desires to bring His restoration or fresh life to things within us. To be honest, in my experience it is often not until afterwards that I can look back and see that His timing was perfect.

It is funny how you don't really know how busy you have been or what a fast pace you have been running at until you stop for a moment and take a deep breath. It is only when you stop and take time to breathe that you can see you may actually have been running at an unhealthy or an unsustainable pace. You may have been overdoing it in certain areas of your life – maybe physically, emotionally, mentally, or maybe all of the above. It is only when you deliberately take time to step off the treadmill of daily life, with all of its differing demands, that

> The truth is that you will never enter into the rest He intends for you to know until you stop and take time to rest and to breathe.

you can see things in a clearer way regarding the actual pace of your life. Then you are able to see the place for any adjustments that may be needed or required.

It turned out that this was certainly one of those moments for me. That morning, and over the next couple of days on the porch of that cabin in the middle of nowhere, I began to just sit and listen. I began to hear the Lord saying to me clearly, 'Before you can experience My restoration you have to come through the doorway of My rest.' It's amazing that the first four letters of both restore and restoration are 'rest'. The truth is that you will never enter into the rest He intends for you to know until you stop and take time to rest and to breathe. It is when you make time to breathe that you actually enter into a more rested state and it is in this rested state where you can hear the Lord clearly. It is here that He can do some of His very best work in your life.

Another very relevant truth is that true rest is only found in Him! Have you ever noticed how you can go away for two weeks somewhere to rest, even somewhere far away and exotic, and you can come back as exhausted as when you left? Why is that? It is because true, meaningful rest is found on the inside of you, not just in having time off or pampering the outside of you. True rest, rest that revives you from the inside out is only found in Him and with Him. It is when you allow Him to position you in His green pastures and lead you beside His still waters that you can experience the restoration of your soul in ways that only He can do. Remember, the invitation of Jesus was not 'Come to Me and I will burn you out and burden you down', rather it was 'Come to Me and I will give you rest, I will give you rest for your weary soul' (Matthew 11:28).

I really want to encourage you to not be so in-sync with this crazy world we live in that you are out of step with God's intended pace and rhythms for your life. Remember that, just as those first followers of Jesus,

> If you create the space He will always meet you there!

we too are in this world but no longer of it (John 17:16). Take time and, if you need to, then make time to pull away from things that are distracting you. Pull away from those things that are stressing you out and take some time to rest with the purpose of knowing the Lord's restoring and reviving hand in your innermost being. I promise you that if you create the space He will always meet you there! Rest was designed by Him and is meant to be an important and valuable part of the lives He has given us to live.

Let's look at the second word the Lord spoke into my life on those first few days and throughout the time I was away, even long after as well: 'breathe'. As I began to meditate on the word 'breathe' I must admit that I thought to myself, 'How difficult is it to understand that? It's simple: we all breathe. It's a part of being alive!' I seem to have breathed fairly successfully for the past fifty-three years. I suppose the real question was: had I? It was then that the Lord began to challenge my understanding of my breathing with statements like: 'Yes, you are breathing, but are you breathing correctly?', 'Are you breathing like I made you to when I made the first man Adam?', 'Are you breathing the breath of the fallen Adam or that of the last Adam: Jesus?'

Okay, so now I was very intrigued, and I did the only thing I knew to do: I turned to the book of Genesis. I wanted to look once again at the verses that were related to the creation of the first man Adam, to see again for myself what God had planned for him when He gave him the ability to breathe.

Let me show you what I discovered on a journey that involved learning to breathe again and learning to breathe correctly. I believe, as we move forward into this book, that God is going to take away breathlessness and hyperventilation in your life and is going to teach you how to breathe in a brand-new way: a way that will affect both who you are and what you do. What the Lord did in me over those next three weeks, and since, was truly life changing and I am believing and praying that He will do the same for you as you continue to read this book.

Oh, how very different the life that God intends for us to know can be from the one we have inherited, made for ourselves or settled for. We are going to look very honestly at this and dare to see it for what it is, we are going to look at the life Adam passed onto us as his natural-born descendants and compare it to the one Jesus has restored for us to know. Like I said, how very different they can be! A very relative comparison was shown to me when we eventually left that cabin in the woods. When our time was up in Upstate New York we began to make our way down to Washington DC to see the White House and other famous sights. To get to Washington DC we had to travel on a road called the New Jersey Turnpike. If you have ever travelled on this road then you will understand exactly what I am saying next. We hit it at a busy time and got stuck in its never-ending traffic. This would not have been so bad if there was something nice to look at but the scenery was terrible. Unlike the beautiful Catskill Mountains which we had just left, or like the Blue Ridge and Smoky Mountains which we would see later on our trip, we were now surrounded by ugly grey industrial buildings, concrete, smog, factories and abandoned cars.

As we sat there in our minibus, which someone had kindly lent us, we looked around at this concrete jungle that was beyond ugly. I reflected back to the forest we had known earlier that morning, the mountains and trees that we had driven through on our way to this infamous interstate. In that moment a great comparison came to me and I had to smile. As I looked into the rear-view mirror, reminding myself of the beautiful countryside we had driven through earlier, with its stunning scenery and tranquillity, I thought to myself, 'That is the life that God made.' Then I looked around at the concrete mess that now surrounded us, the unbreathable air and the cars jammed up almost on top of each other as everyone hurried to be somewhere else, and I thought to myself, 'And here we have the life that Adam made.' Boy, were they different experiences of life, and how my heart pined for what God had made over what Adam had because it was so much better. So it is in life – there is the craziness of life that we have received from Adam that can pollute you and burn you out if you let it, yet there remains a God-designed life for us that we can all know if we want to, which is so superior. The question is: do we want to? Do we want to know what it is to live in a way of life that does not take your breath away but instead causes you to breathe deep, healthy, life-filled breaths that revive us from the inside out?

Are you ready to take this journey of rediscovery with me that I am believing is going to revive you and set a brand-new pace for you to live by? Then take a deep breath. Breathe out, and let's get going.

MY PRAYER FOR YOU

Father, I pray that as we move forward into these thoughts concerning breathing and restoration, that You would cause deep revelations within the heart of every reader to burst forth concerning what You made for them to know and how they can know it here on earth. I pray that you would speak concerning Your breath and the restoration You have made available to know through Your Son. Holy Spirit, would You let truth come to life and speak to every heart, visiting the deepest places within and restoring Your life and well-being. Amen.

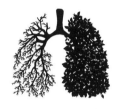

Chapter 2
MADE TO BREATHE

The Rise and Fall of Adam

So let's take a closer look at Adam. Before meeting him, for the sake of setting context please allow me to give a brief overview of the verses which precede the ones that introduce his formation – especially the verses that introduce us to the creator God. When we start reading chapter one of Genesis, the very first book in the Bible which is referred to by some as 'the book of beginnings', we are immediately introduced to the author, the architect and Father of creation by the grand opening declaration 'In the beginning God . . .'.

This statement directly points our attention to God Almighty, the one and only true God. Triune in both existence and expression, having no beginning or end, unlike that which He created. Having no beginning or end. Self-created and self-sustaining, He exists independent of and needing nothing from anyone or anything outside of who He is. With no man able to do anything that would cause Him to be increased, decreased or be sustained in any way, He is God. From Him all things find their origin and through His providence all things continue to exist. Alpha and Omega, beginning and end. Living outside of the restraints of time and space He existed before any timeline of life that we know or judge things by. Before all things and over all things, omniscient, omnipotent and omnipresent. He reigns forever unrivalled and unequalled in His own glory and majesty.

As we continue to read on in chapter one of Genesis we then see this triune God – Father, Son and Holy Spirit – bring forth creation out of void and nothingness. A beautiful demonstration of the unity of the Godhead displayed as the Father, Son and the Holy Spirit, absent of any contention among themselves, create universes and everything we know and experience today. In a wonderful collaboration of 'from Him' (Father), 'through Him' (Jesus) and 'by Him' (Holy Spirit), all things find their beginning in Him. It is then on the eve of day six when we are introduced to His final masterpiece, which He deliberately left until the end so that it could enjoy with him all that He had previously made. This final masterpiece was to be far different and far superior to anything else that God had made before. It is in this moment that we see Adam fashioned, and man was born. As we read on we soon become aware that God made Adam to essentially do one thing: to breathe! In order for us to lay a correct platform for where we are heading together in this book, let us consider further this moment where the first man, Adam, came into existence. Consider also the purposes God had for creating him, and indeed the human race that was in him.

Firstly we must understand that Adam (the name simply means 'man' or 'mankind') existed in the mind of God long before he was ever made. Just as a fully made, ornate vase exists in the mind of a master potter before he ever sits at the wheel to fashion it, so was man and his purpose in God's mind. Just as existence precedes conception concerning us in God's mind today (Jeremiah 1:5) so it was for the first man to be made. Adam was in God's mind and His plans before the dust was ever gathered into the creator's hands to be fashioned. God desired a man, and indeed a mankind, that were made in His image and that carried His distinct likeness so that He could love them and have fellowship with them. To put that in a better way: to love them and to share His life with them. This is the true meaning of fellowship: shared life (the sharing of life with someone). Adam was not made for the purpose of filling any loneliness in God because God had no loneliness, nor was he made to fulfil Him in any way because He was already fully fulfilled in Himself. No, Adam (man) was made to be the object of God's love. Scripture reveals to us clearly that God is love (1 John 4:8), which means that love in its truest and purest form is actually just another way of spelling God's name! Love is not something He does, rather who He is. He does not just express love in His deeds and actions alone, He *is* love!

ADAM'S CREATION AND PURPOSE

Being the very fountain of love, God wanted someone to be able to reveal His love to and lavish His love upon; this was the purpose of Adam (and us) being created. Man was made to know, to experience and to live in His love. Contrary to some opinions of Adam I have heard expressed, Adam was not made to be a slave, an employee or a servant but to be a friend and lover of God. He was brought into being to experience the incredible privilege of sharing life with the eternal God. Though he would not be equal with or ever supersede the position of the beloved Son, Jesus, he was not made to know a lesser standard of life than God but to be a partaker (sharer) of God's very own life. He was created for the most intimate of friendships with God. This was why he carried God's own likeness because God would only be able to relate, at the intimate level He intended to, with someone who was like Him, someone who carried His likeness. This is why, above everything else He created, He made man (humanity) differently. He made Adam not only in His image but also in His likeness. When you look a little closer at chapter one you can also see that everything else which was created over those six days was formed or came into existence by God speaking it into being with His words. It was only with man that we see Him bend down and fashion something with His own hands and then breathe His own life into its nostrils.

He was brought into being to experience the incredible privilege of sharing life with the eternal God.

In summary, God made man in His image and likeness so that He could pour out and lavish His love on them and share His breath (*zoe* life) with them.

Therefore, man was made for a much higher purpose than anything else that God made. In fact, the reality is that everything else He made was merely the environment that would house and fulfil that which He would truly adore: man.

When I think about this I am reminded of my own five children and how at different times we had to buy them pets; at one time or another every child wants one or momentarily believes they need one, don't they? But, before you get the pet you must take time and spend money to create the environment that will house them. If it is a hamster or mouse then you buy a cage, a water bottle, a feeding tray, bedding, an exercise wheel and anything else they can convince you that the pet needs. It's the same with a fish: you first buy a fish tank, stones, ornaments, plants – the list goes on and on. But think about it for a moment: those things aren't the main focus of your pleasure and passion, are they? Why? Their purpose is only to house or contain, or provide a healthy environment for, the pet that you are bringing home. It is the pet that your children will (hopefully) love, appreciate and care for. It is the pet that they will cuddle and adore, not its bedding, food or water bottle. In the same way, in the opening pages of Genesis, we see the creator God make everything that was needed to accommodate, bless and fascinate the man He had in His heart to bring into being. Did God delight in what He had made? Yes, I believe He may have delighted in it to some degree, but He also knew He had made it all for a higher purpose.

Then in chapter one, once everything had been made and was correctly in position, we see Him create that which was to be the delight of His heart, that which would know the intimacy of relationship with Him like nothing else could: man! Let's take a look at the moment when Adam is created in Genesis 2:

> *This is the account of the heavens and the earth when they were created, when the LORD God made the earth and the heavens. Now no shrub had yet appeared on the earth and no plant had yet sprung up, for the LORD God had not sent rain on the earth and there was no one to work the ground, but streams came up from the earth and watered the whole surface of the ground.* ***Then the LORD God formed a man from the dust of the ground and breathed into his nostrils the breath of life, and the man became a living being.*** *Now the LORD God had planted a garden in the east, in Eden; and there he put the man he had formed.*
> *Genesis 2:4-8 (NIV, emphasis mine)*

As previously mentioned in these verses we see everything ready and awaiting the arrival of the man. Everything is now in position and ready to burst forth with glorious life, the shrubs and plants are quietly waiting with patience to express the colours and many different scents contained within them. But we see God had not yet pressed the play button on the paradise He had created, allowing it to burst forth with life – why? Because there was not yet a man made and positioned to manage it.

It is at this moment we can see God bend down to form man with His own hands from the dust of the ground, fashioning man as a master potter would a prize pot. He must have held the formed clay for a while in His hands and looked intently at it to see if it was everything He desired it to be, to see if the still lifeless model He held carried His image and likeness precisely. It was then when He was fully satisfied with His workmanship He did the thing that would change everything for the clay in His hands and the creation He had spoken into being: He breathed His own life and Spirit (*ru'ach*) into its nostrils. Suddenly a heart began to beat within the chest of the model, blood began to pump, veins and arteries opened and began to flow this wonderful new God-life around its body. That which was previously just an inanimate object, that which was once just common dust of the earth suddenly became living cells, carefully knitted together and packed with unique DNA. Then came the moment when the now fully alive first man opened his eyes and beheld the face of his maker and life-giver. Without any past or history, the fully formed man who was fashioned by the very hands of God for the purpose of relationship and intimacy with God, breathed his first breath and tasted within every cell and fibre of who he was, God's very own life.

Man had now been made, indeed fearfully and wonderfully made (Psalm 139:14).

How long this life-giving moment of first encounter and embrace between the creator God and His perfect creation lasted, no one can know, but how they must have marvelled, talked and walked together in the paradise that God had created for that very purpose, a paradise that had been specifically made to contain and house this perfect love relationship. Then, in verse 19 we see God bring to Adam the other living things that He had made, the animals and birds, for him to name and give them their identity. Unintimidated, they worked together in paradise like a father and a child in the Father's workshop, enjoying one shared life together. As we continue reading we can see it is when Adam is giving God's creation individual identities and purposes that the Lord recognises Adam's desire and need for a helpmate. So He caused woman to be taken from man and then joined to him again in shared life with each other and with Himself, this being the very first expression of the three-corded strand of marriage, spoken of in Ecclesiastes 4:12.

POSITIONED TO RULE AND REIGN

His life was now their life and without ever having to think about it they drew on it daily, never knowing any other way to live or exist. It is also at this point when we see God set the man and woman He had created into the Garden of Eden. Their purpose was to manage and tend it, to rule and reign over all that God had created and had now activated by His Word. Yes, that's right, Adam was made to work, but not like the work some of you know or may have known, if your work is something you just tolerate to get money and do not enjoy. Adam loved what he did and found total fulfilment in it. He was not stressed out, burned out or mentally fried by what he did; rather he was totally fulfilled, empowered and blessed. We get a further endorsement of this fact a little later on in chapter two.

> *The LORD God took the man and put him in the Garden of Eden to work it and take care of it.*
> **Genesis 2:15 (NIV)**

Also, if we flip back to chapter one again we get another beautiful picture of Adam and Eve being positioned to rule and reign with all authority in God's created paradise, called Eden.

> *God blessed them and said to them, 'Be fruitful and increase in number; fill the earth and subdue it. Rule over the fish in the sea and the birds in the sky and over every living creature that moves on the ground.' Then God said, 'I give you every seed-bearing plant on the face of the whole earth and every tree that has fruit with seed in it. They will be yours for food. And to all the beasts of the earth and all the birds in the sky and all the*

creatures that move along the ground—everything that has the breath of life in it—I give every green plant for food.' And it was so. God saw all that he had made, and it was very good. And there was evening, and there was morning—the sixth day.
Genesis 1:28-31 (NIV)

So Adam and Eve now had all authority and charge over everything else that had been created, every living thing was under their authority. They truly ruled and reigned with God. They had everything they could ever need or desire, as they lived each day under the divine protection and providence of the Father of creation.

Though they found great purpose and fulfilment in working, this was always secondary to the primary purpose they had been made for which was fellowship. They were made to simply enjoy each day, sharing life with God. God was with them and they were with Him; we get a glimpse of God walking in the cool of the day looking for them just after they had eaten the fruit of disobedience in Genesis 3, but I don't believe this was a one-off event that occurred after they had blown it, rather something that they knew on a daily basis. They walked with God and knew Him in their day each and every day. Life in the garden was indeed heavenly, beyond anything we could possibly imagine. They worked in a stress-free way, enjoying the fruits of their labour and daily walking with God, drawing upon and sharing His life. Oh, what a beautiful picture this creates in our imaginations, if we take a moment to ponder on it. They wanted for nothing, feared nothing, were anxious for nothing, their breathing perfectly in time with His breathing because they simply shared His life. Life was good, life was everything God has made it to be!

BUT THEN . . .

But then, as we know, everything changes when an act of deliberate disobedience is committed and we witness what we most often term 'the fall of man'. Suddenly this beautiful picture we have painted of God and man coexisting in shared life in the paradise of Eden, comes to a sudden halt. Sin brutally enters in like a sudden car-crash, bringing with it the death and separation which God warned would have to take place if they touched the forbidden tree.

Most of you know this part of the story very well but, if not, then please take a moment to read Genesis 3:1-10 in order to familiarise yourself with it. To briefly highlight what happens, the devil comes into the perfect picture and tempts Adam and Eve to sin. He tests their hearts by tempting them to put their will in a higher place than God's will, to do what they wanted instead of what God wanted for them. The devil deceives them into disobeying God's clear command, to not eat of one tree in the garden: the tree of the knowledge of good and evil. First, satan entices Eve by sowing seemingly harmless questions about God and His Word into her heart, convincing her that she was somehow missing out on something.

Causing her to think that God was somehow holding out on them and that there was more they did not know about, but could have if they wanted. In her state of deception she deliberately eats of the forbidden fruit and then convinces Adam to do the same. By eating the forbidden fruit they stepped out of obedience into disobedience and sin entered them. They had now become contaminated with the treasonous nature of the one who had tempted them. In that moment they became unholy, and God, being just, would then have to carry out the consequence of which He had previously warned them.

It is vital that we understand that He never stopped loving them! He had to remove them now from Eden and from shared life with Himself, because the nature within them had changed. It was now contaminated and unholy, which meant they could not remain in the union with God that they had known. The unholy could no longer be joined or share life as it had done with the holy, which is what God is. Just as He is love, He is holy. Please allow me to underline once again: He did not fall out of love with them, because God's love is not like that. God could never and would never stop loving them and would later demonstrate this love by paying love's greatest price to redeem (purchase) them back to Himself (John 15:13).

SEPARATED FROM HIS LIFE

We now find ourselves in Genesis 3 and as the story

unfolds further we see them confronted by God and escorted out of Eden. The entrance back into the garden now guarded by an angel with a flaming sword. This maintained that there could be no return through that door. This was because God said they could no longer have access to the tree of life, the spiritual life they had shared with Him before. Everything had changed because of the rebellious choice they had made; they had now become removed and barred from Eden.

> *The LORD God made garments of skin for Adam and his wife and clothed them. And the LORD God said, 'The man has now become like one of us, knowing good and evil. He must not be allowed to reach out his hand and take also from the tree of life and eat, and live forever.' So the LORD God banished him from the Garden of Eden to work the ground from which he had been taken. After he drove the man out, he placed on the east side of the Garden of Eden cherubim and a flaming sword flashing back and forth to guard the way to the tree of life.*
> **Genesis 3:21-24 (NIV)**

Oh, how everything had suddenly and radically changed for Adam and Eve in that one moment. Now they stood on the other side of the entrance gate into Eden, the spiritual life they had known. How they must have longed to relive that moment again and not eat the fruit offered them by satan; how their hearts must have longed for what they had with God before their fall or separation. Suddenly, the shared life they had once known with God was no longer in them. They were still breathing, but it was a different type of breath. It felt so different. It was now the breath of mere existence and not the *zoe* life of God they had once known. The breath they now breathed was mortal breath. Before their breath had been eternal; now they had to live in the independence that they had chosen by their disobedience

> Adam and Eve were sentenced, by their own doing, to know a life of mere existence. They would now know pain, anxiety, fear and every other result of the sin nature that was now activated in them.

and life would be so very different to what they had known before. They were now sentenced, by their own doing, to know a life of mere existence. They would now know pain, anxiety, fear and every other result of the sin nature that was now activated in them. Listen to how different life was for them in chapter three compared to the life they had known in chapter two:

To Adam he said, 'Because you listened to your wife and ate fruit from the tree about which I commanded you, "You must not eat from it," cursed is the ground because of you; through painful toil you will eat food from it all the days of your life. It will produce thorns

and thistles for you, and you will eat the plants of the field. By the sweat of your brow you will eat your food until you return to the ground, since from it you were taken; for dust you are and to dust you will return.'
Genesis 3:17-19 (NIV)

Now there would be thorns, now there would be sweat, now they would experience a cursed ground instead of a blessed one. Now their provision and protection was down to them, it was in their own hands. They had lost the ease of breathing that they had known when they were joined to the life of God. Now what they had instead was the breathless pants of a fallen mortal humanity that was responsible for itself. Now as I said before they would know fear that they had never known, worry, anxiety and all of those other things that can take your breath away, and make you feel like you are hyperventilating. These were now daily things they had to deal with as they merely existed together – still very loved by God but unplugged from His *zoe* life. Oh how the picture now was so very different to the one they had once known. What hope did they and the unborn human race within them have?

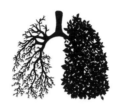

Chapter 3

GOOD NEWS,
GOD HAD A PLAN!

As we left the last chapter everything looked bleak, lifeless and hopeless for Adam and Eve and for the fallen human race within their loins. Whether you look at Adam (which simply means 'man') as a singular person or as mankind, a separation was now in place that would always cause – both consciously or unconsciously – an inner craving for something better they had once tasted and known. As it has often been said: within every person there truly is a missing God-shaped piece that only clicks back into its position when they are rejoined to God.

So back to our storyline: everything now looks hopeless! But wait a moment – let us not forget that God had a plan! There is a gospel, or as we know it more commonly, 'good news'. Even though He had to be just and righteous by removing the fallen man from Eden, He would also be loving and redemptive in restoring them back because, like I said before, He never stopped loving them! Restoration through redemption was always on His mind even as He was leading them out of Eden; though He could not use the door they had left by in the fullness of time, He would provide another door which would enable a fallen humanity to come back home and a now spiritually dead humanity to come back to fullness of life. That door, of course, was His only beloved Son: Jesus.

> Restoration through redemption was always on His mind

> *But when the fullness of the time had come, God*
> *sent forth His Son, born of a woman, born under*
> *the law, to redeem those who were under the law,*
> *that we might receive the adoption as sons.*
> ***Galatians 4:4-5 (NKJV)***
>
> *I am the door. If anyone enters by Me, he will be*
> *saved, and will go in and out and find pasture.*
> *The thief does not come except to steal, and to kill,*
> *and to destroy. I have come that they may have life,*
> *and that they may have it more abundantly.*
> ***John 10:9-10 (NKJV)***

Notice here that the verse above does not just speak about Jesus being the provided door for the safe return of fallen humanity but also that Jesus came to give life, and not just life but life in abundance. It's interesting that the word used for life in these verses is the Greek word *zoe* which is different from the normal word that we use for life – *bios*[1] – referring to us being born naturally into this life. The word *zoe* means 'the God kind of life' or as others have translated it 'the very state of life that God enjoys Himself'. Strong's Concordance defines it this way:

i. of the absolute fullness of life, both essential and ethical, which belongs to God.
ii. life real and genuine, a life active and vigorous,

---

1 Strong's reference: 979

devoted to God, blessed, in the portion even in this world of those who put their trust in Christ.[2]

So what Jesus was actually saying here was that He came to give us life, 'the God kind of life'. He came to restore us to a state of being that had been lost to us through Adam's disobedience. Jesus came to redeem a lost humanity by repairing the breach that caused it, by the first Adam. Why Jesus? It was an eternal perfect man who lost everything for humanity and sentenced them to a death of mere existence, so it could only be an eternal perfect man who could restore them and bring them back to the fullness of life which they were originally made to know. The only one who was eternal and perfect to that degree and beyond was Jesus. Think about how much Father God loved us that He would send His only son to save and redeem us?

For God so [greatly] loved and dearly prized the world, that He [even] gave His [One and] only begotten Son, so that whoever believes and trusts in Him [as Savior] shall not perish, but have eternal life. For God did not send the Son into the world to judge and condemn the world [that is, to initiate the final judgment of the world], but that the world might be saved through Him.
John 3:16-17 (AMP)

2 James Strong, Strong's Exhaustive Concordance of the Bible, (Hendrickson Publishers, Inc., 2007), G2222.

So the good news (gospel) for us is that God's divine plan of redemption would restore His fallen creation back to its original pre-fallen state. This is what we commonly call a one hundred per cent redemption. You may have heard this terminology used by pastors and Christian speakers before but have you grasped the incredible ramifications it has? When we say we believe in a one hundred per cent redemption, we are saying that we believe that everything which was lost or ruined by the first Adam has been restored and fixed by the second or last Adam: Jesus! Think about that for a moment and let it move from mere knowledge to a revelation breathed by the Spirit, so deep within you that it will define you for the rest of your days. Jesus did not achieve a partial success, it was not a ninety-five per cent redemption that leaves Him now relying on us to help Him out with the remaining five per cent. This would mean that what the devil did through the first Adam was greater than what God did through Jesus. No! That is just not true. What God did through

> It was an eternal perfect man who lost everything for humanity and sentenced them to a death of mere existence, so it could only be an eternal perfect man who could restore them and bring them back to the fullness of life which they were originally made to know.

Jesus totally restored us and, as a matter of fact, He overpaid the debt that was on our lives so there would be no more bills or demands for us to have to pay!

UNDERSTANDING THE TWO ADAMS

It is important at this point to realise that the Bible acknowledges two Adams, not one. For us to understand the fullness of our redemption, this must also be revelation to us. Remember what we are saying is that the last Adam (Jesus) totally repaired the damage done by the first Adam.

> *But Christ has indeed been raised from the dead, the firstfruits of those who have fallen asleep. For since death came through a man, the resurrection of the dead comes also through a man. **For as in Adam all die, so in Christ all will be made alive**.*
> *1 Corinthians 15:20-22 (NIV, emphasis mine)*

Look now at how Paul expands on this thought in verses 44-49 of the same chapter.

> *If there is a natural body, there is also a spiritual body. So it is written: '**The first man Adam became a living being**'; the last Adam, a life-giving spirit. The spiritual did not come first, but the natural, and after that the spiritual. The first man was of the dust of the earth; the second man is of heaven. As was the earthly man, so are those who are of the earth; and as is the heavenly man, so also are those*

who are of heaven. And just as we have borne the
image of the earthly man, so shall we bear the
image of the heavenly man.
1 Corinthians 15:44-49 (NIV, emphasis mine)

Paul puts it so simply when he speaks of that which is born of the earth and that which is born of the Spirit. All of humanity died in the first Adam but then comes alive again (to true life) through new birth in the last Adam, Jesus. To expand this thought further let's look at what Paul teaches in the book of Romans, on that same truth. Please do not speed-read this, but rather take time to slowly read and digest the content of it because it contains truly life-shaping truth for your life and walk with God.

Therefore, just as through one man sin entered the
world, and death through sin, and thus death spread
to all men, because all sinned—(For until the law
sin was in the world, but sin is not imputed when
there is no law. Nevertheless death reigned from Adam
to Moses, even over those who had not sinned
according to the likeness of the transgression of Adam,
who is a type of Him who was to come. But the free
gift is not like the offense. ***For if by the one man's***
offense many died, much more the grace of God
and the gift by the grace of the one Man, Jesus
Christ, abounded to many. *And the gift is not like*
that which came through the one who sinned. For
the judgment which came from one offense resulted

in condemnation, but the free gift which came from many offenses resulted in justification. **For if by the one man's offense death reigned through the one, much more those who receive abundance of grace and of the gift of righteousness will reign in life through the One, Jesus Christ.)** *Therefore, as through one man's offense judgment came to all men, resulting in condemnation, even so through one Man's righteous act the free gift came to all men, resulting in justification of life.* **For as by one man's disobedience many were made sinners, so also by one Man's obedience many will be made righteous.** *Romans 5:12-19 (NKJV, emphasis mine)*

Notice how deliberately repetitive Paul is concerning the subject of what both Adams produced for humanity. He did this on purpose to underline the fact that what started with one Adam, ended with the other Adam. We can try to describe what happened in and through them in a variety of different ways, but it always leaves us with the same conclusion. The first Adam tied a death-sentence knot for humanity; the last Adam – Jesus – untied that knot. The first Adam got us thrown out of the party (Eden); the last Adam brings us back in.

As a younger man, who was sadly not following after God, I was often asked to leave parties at various occasions. This was normally because of my own bad behaviour, so even though I was being removed I felt some justice in it: I was paying for what I had done. However, there were a couple of times that I was removed from parties and clubs because of my reputation; I had not actually done what they had accused me of, but I was blamed for the acts of another. I can remember being enraged at this apparent lack of justice in those times. I would argue with the man on the door, telling him that I had not done what they said, that I deserved to be in the party and not outside of it. Basically, my declarations were: 'It wasn't me, this is not fair!' To be honest, this is how I also felt initially when I began to read what happened to humanity in and through the first Adam. I remember thinking to myself: 'That's not fair: he ate the apple, I didn't!' Why should I suffer because of His disobedience? Why did his consequences become my consequences? I didn't do it, I was not there!

The whole time I was obviously totally overlooking all of the sin that was in my life, sin that was my fault which was the product of the sin nature which was within me, because of my union to it through my first birth. It was the inherent sin that I had an issue with. Why was I being punished for someone else's wrong-doing? The answer is simple: as Adam stood in Eden, the human race was in him too, and he fully represented it. Again, whether you believe Adam to be a singular man or to mean a more plural mankind, the fact still remains: he was the representative of the original creation. All of the human race was in him, even if they were yet unborn. There was no plan of producing another race of people, contrary to the mere theories of evolution.

Humanity's origins were in a created being who was formed by the hands of the creator God. Just like a bookmark in a book: wherever the book goes the bookmark goes with it. Whatever happens to the book, the bookmark is a part of it, because it is in the book. It was the exactly same for us: we were in Adam when he fell, so we fell with him.

This seems unfair, but concerning our restoration, it is also a wonderful thing. It is in fact the simplicity of this that makes our redemption so easy to grasp. If, in one perfect man, we all sinned and were separated from God and His life, how many perfect men does it take to restore us? That's right, only one! That is why Jesus was the only one who could redeem us; He was the only perfect man. Eternally perfect, He was born of a woman by immaculate conception and His Father was God. This being the case, He carried none of the imperfections or sin nature of a fallen man: He was perfect in every way. From birth to the cross He lived a sinless life. He was tempted in every way, as we are, but He sinned not. He could not sin not even once because He was to be our redeeming sacrifice and He had to be a perfect sacrifice, as it was in the Old Testament, a lamb without any spot or blemish.

THE DIVINE EXCHANGE

Then, at the cross, we see Him take our place as He takes upon Himself the sin of Adam and of all humanity past, present and future. In a single act of obedient redeeming sacrifice, He activated a divine exchange that would affect both those who lived before the cross and all those who would come after. A divine exchange that would settle the original debt that was set into place by the first Adam, releasing humanity, who God had never stopped loving, back into knowing the true life (*zoe*) that He intended for them to know from the beginning. This divine exchange took place on a cross two thousand years ago, yet it affects all men. I love the way Paul puts it in 2 Corinthians when he implores us to come into reconciliation with God:

> *God made him who had no sin to be sin for us, so that in him we might become the righteousness of God.*
> *2 Corinthians 5:21 (NIV)*

Can you see the exchange? Can you see how you and I benefited from it? The law of exchange works like this: whenever something is exchanged, both parties involved leave the moment of exchange with something different to what they came with. This is exactly what happened at the cross and becomes activated or vital in the life of a person when they place their faith in Jesus. Two thousand years ago Jesus approached the cross – sinless, righteous and joined to the life of His Father. Whereas we (mankind) approached it sinful because of the disqualifying inherent nature in us, not just the things we have done. We were unrighteous and dead to the life of God which we were created to know. At the cross He substituted Himself and took our place, taking upon Himself our sin (both inherent and self-achieved), our guilt and our shame. He received the full judgment for our sin and took upon Himself the full punishment for the demands of that judgment. With the one-time shedding of His perfect blood, He fully paid the debt that was upon us, for all time. His single act of obedience by going to the cross, totally wiped away the act of disobedience committed in the garden by the first Adam.

But wait a moment – we said it was an exchange, but we have only spoken about one party involved: Him. This is where it gets even better for us. You see, as He became sin for us, at the same moment of exchange, His innocent right standing with His Father became ours. Think about it: we did nothing to enter into death and disqualification, we were just born. In the same way we have to do nothing to enter into qualification and restoration except be born, or as we more commonly term it, be born again, and this comes only through placing faith in Jesus. It is at the moment of our new birth that our lives are taken (snatched out) from the kingdom (dominion) of darkness and translated (brought back into) the kingdom of the Son He loves (Colossians 1:13). It's at this moment of new birth that God takes our life out of the first Adam and places us in Christ (the last Adam). It is at this moment when we are placed in Jesus that new life begins for us and we start to breathe again, fresh life. Not the dead breath of mere existence we knew before, but now the breath of abundant life that Jesus promised we would know. Now clothed in robes of white we don't deserve we no longer wear the sin-stained garments we once did; rather we have been clothed in garments of white that are whiter than the snow.

MORE THAN 100%

But wait a moment: was it really a one-hundred-percent redemption? Do we just see Jesus restore us to the place that the first Adam knew before His fall, Eden? That would certainly be enough, wouldn't it? But Jesus did much, much more than that! You see, Jesus did not just restore to us what we had lost in Adam but He also added to it and gave us what Adam, as far as we know, had never known or experienced. The Bible says that through Jesus we have now been 'seated . . . in heavenly realms (places) in Christ Jesus' (Ephesians 2:6, NIV). Think about that: again, as far as we know, Adam never knew heaven; the Bible revealed that God walked with him on the earth (Eden) He had created for him. Yet when we are born again, the Bible reveals that we are 'seated in heavenly realms (places) in Christ' and also that we can now know the throne room of God (Hebrews 4:16). You see, Jesus did not just redeem us back to what Adam had known at creation

> Jesus did not just restore to us what we had lost in Adam but He also added to it and gave us what Adam, as far as we know, had never known or experienced.

but He actually took us further and higher. He positioned us in heavenly places! He took us higher, to where Adam had never been. In Christ we can know the quality of life that Adam first knew in Eden, this being obviously the key point of this book, but we can also now know and have access to what he had never experienced. Again, this must leave us thinking: 'How much greater was what God did through Jesus than what the enemy did through Adam!' So much greater; through our redemption Jesus does not just restore our breathing back to an Eden way of breathing that Adam first knew, He also gives us access and position that was beyond the experience of the first man, Adam. Thank You, Jesus, for Your perfect salvation – it is truly perfect!

> *But God, who is rich in mercy, because of His great love with which He loved us, even when we were dead in trespasses, made us alive together with Christ (by grace you have been saved),* **and raised us up together, and made us sit together in the heavenly places in Christ Jesus,** *that in the ages to come He might show the exceeding riches of His grace in His kindness toward us in Christ Jesus.*
> *Ephesians 2:4-7 (NKJV, emphasis mine)*

> *Let us therefore come boldly to the throne of grace, that we may obtain mercy and find grace to help in time of need.*
> *Hebrews 4:16 (NKJV)*

As we leave this chapter, allow me to underline again that everything which has now been made available to us by the perfect finished work of Christ, is available to all of mankind. But it can only be accessed through new birth (being born again), so having a correct understanding of our new birth is vitally important. Let's now take a deeper look at what it is to be born again, spiritually regenerated, born from above!

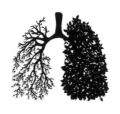

Chapter 4

BORN AGAIN TO
BREATHE AGAIN

*H*aving now taken the time to lay a strong foundation of how we lost our breath and what God has done to restore His breath (life) to us we can now look in a more significant way at the key ingredient to getting our breath back, our new birth.

As we have seen a number of times so far in our journey together, it was the moment that Adam left the Garden of Eden that he (we) died and stopped living from a union with God's divine life. Instead we were plunged into a life sentence of mere existence. In that moment when Adam left Eden, it was like he left a womb, was born and started to breathe for himself for the very first time. Just as a midwife used to smack the bottom of a baby to start it breathing on its own, so the doorpost of Eden did this to Adam's at his exit. On leaving Eden he had become disconnected from the joined life of his parent and instead started to breathe the self-initiated breath of self-existence. A divine umbilical cord had been cut and Adam now began to breathe his own breath, the breath of a mortal man.

Let us think a little differently about this, by looking at it now through the lens of our redemption. What if, when a person believes in Jesus and is born again, they are actually spiritually born again? What if, the moment they come into Christ by faith, they actually come through Jesus back into union with the Father and shared life with Him? They enter back into the 'Eden state of being' that Adam originally knew before his fall. What if Eden, for us, is not a physical place far, far away that we must be dead physically in order to experience, but a state of being that we can experience not just in the life to come but here and now as well? Take a moment to breathe in and think about that! What if, what Jesus did for us restored us more than we have yet realised or perceived?

So, what did Jesus mean when He said a person must be born again?

> *Now there was a Pharisee, a man named Nicodemus who was a member of the Jewish ruling council. He came to Jesus at night and said, 'Rabbi, we know that you are a teacher who has come from God. For no one could perform the signs you are doing if God were not with him.' Jesus replied, '**Very truly I tell**

you, no one can see the kingdom of God unless they are born again.' 'How can someone be born when they are old?' Nicodemus asked. 'Surely they cannot enter a second time into their mother's womb to be born!' Jesus answered, **'Very truly I tell you, no one can enter the kingdom of God unless they are born of water and the Spirit.** Flesh gives birth to flesh, but the Spirit gives birth to spirit. You should not be surprised at my saying, "You must be born again." The wind blows wherever it pleases. You hear its sound, but you cannot tell where it comes from or where it is going. So it is with everyone born of the Spirit.'*
John 3:1-8 (NIV, emphasis mine)

In these very well-known passages we are introduced to Nicodemus, a renowned religious leader. We see him come to Jesus by night to ask Him questions regarding salvation and the kingdom that had, though he was a religious leader, remained unanswered within him. Jesus' response to his questions did not seem very deep, but they were truly profound answers that Nicodemus and, indeed, every one of us must gain a deeper understanding or revelation of. Jesus' response to this earnest seeker of truth was simply: 'you

What if, when a person believes in Jesus and is born again, they are actually spiritually born again?

must be born again'. Just as flesh gives birth to flesh (natural things), so spirit gives birth to spirit (spiritual things). The natural existence that we all know is a product of the flesh, but the spiritual new creation that we are invited to know is the result of the Spirit (breath of God), and a person must be born of the Spirit. Other translations say this in different ways but they all mean the same thing. One says: 'born anew', another says that you must be 'born from above' – the essence being that coming into the new life that Jesus has provided for you is not a matter of mere mental assent or behaviour modification but rather it is a new birth experience where you, through Christ alone, can come alive again to the *zoe* life (breath) of God, with our only involvement in the whole process being to believe (have faith).

THE BIRTH OF THE NEW CREATION

To be born again is such an interesting concept. It reveals that faith in Christ and the salvation that He secured for us by His death, burial and resurrection causes a rebirth in the life of the one who believes. Here, an old existence completely dies and moves aside for a brand-new one that it brings into being the day of the new creation, for the person who has believed. This, of course, reminds us of another well-known statement made by Paul in 2 Corinthians.

Therefore, if anyone is in Christ, he is a new creation; old things have passed away; behold, all things have

become new.
2 Corinthians 5:17 (NKJV)

Notice that Paul refers to the old you as 'passed away', not modified, adapted or repaired. The only time we normally use the terminology 'passed away' is in reference to death and its finality. The example being that we stand around the graveside at a funeral and hear the minister leading the funeral say something along the lines of 'Brother Fred has passed away'. What does he mean by that statement? He means that Fred's life is now over, Fred is gone, that you will never experience Brother Fred in this life again. This is the very meaning that Paul was using regarding us, when he speaks of old things passing away and all things becoming new. Another translation, the New International Version, puts it even simpler: 'the old has gone, the new is here'.

You see, when a person comes through Jesus into the salvation He has provided, they do so by identification. By this I mean that by faith they identify with what Jesus did at the cross and see themselves in Him in all that transpired. In doing this they no longer have to provide their own death to find new life, rather they partake, by faith, in His death and also His burial and resurrection. They also come into the newness of life that was the other side of the tomb that He knew. Just as we passed through Adam into death and separation, so now, through new birth, we pass through Christ into newness of life. It's your identifying, by faith, with what happened at the cross two thousand years ago which causes you to become a full beneficiary of the benefits of what He achieved.

For a deeper understanding of this powerful reality I encourage you to dedicate some time to reading Romans chapter 6 and, as you do, ask the Holy Spirit to open it up to you in a fresh way, to give you eyes of revelation. As He does, you will see so clearly that it was not just Jesus who died on the cross that day, but you died with Him. He did not just die for you, but as you. It was not just Jesus who was buried, your 'old man' was buried with Him, and it was not just Jesus who rose from the dead to newness of life but you rose with Him! Not just in regard to the life to come one day (heaven), but also here on earth. The very moment you prayed the prayer and called on His name as your saviour, He saved you like He promised He would (Romans 10:13). Sound too good to be true? Then read this brief excerpt from Romans 6 to see that it is true, it is the greatest of news, and it is here and it is now.

Or do you not know that as many of us as were baptized into Christ Jesus were baptized into His death? Therefore we were buried with Him through baptism into death, that just as Christ was raised from the dead by the glory of the Father, even so we also should walk in newness of life. For if we have been united together in the likeness of His death, certainly we also shall be in the likeness of His

resurrection, knowing this, that our old man was
crucified with Him, that the body of sin might be
done away with, that we should no longer be slaves
of sin. For he who has died has been freed from
sin. Now if we died with Christ, we believe that
we shall also live with Him, knowing that Christ,
having been raised from the dead, dies no more.
Death no longer has dominion over Him. For the
death that He died, He died to sin once for all; but
the life that He lives, He lives to God. Likewise you
also, reckon yourselves to be dead indeed to sin, but
alive to God in Christ Jesus our Lord.
Romans 6:3-11 (NKJV)

So, why is understanding that you are now a new creation so important to you breathing differently – or should I say, correctly? Simple, until you know that you are dead to your old existence (old man), the one you had in Adam, you can't fully accept that you are now alive to your new life in Christ. Think about it: your death was crucial to your new life. God could not lay life on top of life; there had to be a death. To provide new breath (life) for you, He had to finalise the old you. Otherwise, it would merely be resuscitation. No, He had to stop you breathing the old breath so that you could then breathe His new breath. And nothing is more final that would enable the success of this than death. You were never meant to be some kind of half-alive, spiritual zombie – not fully alive because you were not fully dead! You were meant to be someone who is fully alive in the life of God because you know you fully died in Christ – this death in Him being the key that enables the new life He has given you to properly begin. Sadly, many Christians today never enjoy the full life that Father God has provided for them because they have never 'walked through the corridor' of their death correctly. First we fully die in Him, so that we then fully live in Him.

Both Jesus and Lazarus demonstrate for us that before true resurrection can take place, a death and burial have to first be established. This is what God did for you through His Son. He provided you the death and burial you need to be able to leave the mere flesh-born existence of a fallen Adam behind and experience the Spirit-born life that He always destined for you to know. The good news is you do not have to provide a death to achieve newness of life; He provided one for you, and it is that death that we enter into, and come through by faith, in Christ alone.

> The good news is you do not have to provide a death to achieve newness of life; He provided one for you, and it is that death that we enter into, and come through by faith, in Christ alone.

So let me say again, to avoid any possible confusion: when you are born again, the old creation, the one born in Adam, completely passes away, and the new creation that you become, breathes its first true breath. Like it was in the moment we spoke of when Adam first opened his eyes after receiving the breath of God in the garden, so it is with us at our new birth: we come alive with His life now in us and we can experience sharing His life with Him, as Adam originally did.

NOW ALIVE IN CHRIST

At the start of this chapter we spoke of Adam, the first man, experiencing a birth-like experience in his fall that caused him to be unplugged from God's life, the only life he had ever known, and how he was forced to breathe for himself, the breath of mere existence. I want you to now reverse this process to see more fully what the Lord did through His Son in redeeming (rebirthing) us back to Himself. In this aspect I call our salvation a 'reverse birth manoeuvre'. When a person comes to Christ they are taken, by God, out of Adam and placed into Jesus. They are now 'In Christ' and entitled to the many benefits recorded in God's Word for those who are 'In Christ'. It's at this moment that they actually

> When a person comes to Christ they are taken, by God, out of Adam and placed into Jesus. They are now 'In Christ' and entitled to the many benefits recorded in God's Word for those who are 'In Christ'.

stop merely existing and are re-joined, by a divine umbilical cord, to God; they are spiritually re-joined to Him. It is at this moment that the human and the divine of fallen man are reconnected and the life (*zoe*) that Jesus promised He would give them becomes theirs as they begin to breathe in a new way, the same breath that Adam knew prior to his fall. The new creation at his birth becomes rejoined to God and becomes a partaker of His divine life. Look at how Peter endorses this reality in his second letter:

> *Simon Peter, a bondservant and apostle of Jesus Christ, To those who have obtained like precious faith with us by the righteousness of our God and Savior Jesus Christ: Grace and peace be multiplied to you in the knowledge of God and of Jesus our Lord, as His divine power has given to us all things that pertain to life and godliness, through the knowledge of Him who called us by glory and virtue, by which have been given to us exceedingly great and precious promises,* ***that through these you may be partakers of the divine nature, having escaped the corruption that is in the world through lust.***
> *2 Peter 1:1-4 (NKJV, emphasis mine)*

In the new creation we have escaped the corruption that is in the world by dying to the sin nature that was connected to us in Adam that causes it. We still have a human nature, just as Jesus did, but the sin nature we once knew has been replaced with a divinely connected one. These things are present tense, not future tense. They have been dealt with, and you have now been joined again to the nature of God in Christ.

I like the way this was summed up in a recent Bible course module we were teaching in our Bible school:

In Genesis 1:26-28 we see that the human race was God's idea and creation; He blessed it and had a glorious plan for it. It is not our humanity which must be rejected or escaped from, but the sin nature which has corrupted our humanity and stunted it. Through Jesus, in whom the human and divine natures are re-joined, we can escape the corruption that spoils our humanity and share in the divine nature of God. Our goal is not to reject our humanity or somehow strip ourselves of it, as if we could only reach perfection apart from being human. God's plan has always been to redeem our humanity, bringing it to its full potential, perfecting it, glorifying it, and raising it to a whole new level. This has already happened in the man Jesus and is the final destiny of all who follow Him.

It goes on to say:

It is in the person of Jesus Christ that we see God's ultimate purpose of reconciliation revealed and accomplished. The result of the Fall of man (Genesis

3:1-24) is that the entire human race was alienated
from God, set at odds against Him, and made His
enemies. Jesus came to bring about reconciliation
between God and man, reuniting heaven and earth.
This reconciliation and reunification come together
in Him, as the human and divine natures work
together in harmony to do away with the division
between God and man, heaven and earth.[3]

Think about it, if His Spirit and life are now yours, then so is His nature. Just as the nature of a vine flows into the branch, producing the fruit it desires, fruit that is true to the DNA of the vine, so it is with us. Now that we have been joined back to His divine life (vine), His nature becomes again ours. His life becomes again ours. Now all He wants us to do is remain connected and to draw upon that life daily, to 'suck His sap', to breathe His breath, or however else you would like to put it. As we do, we will live out of the life He now provides for us to know, living in the blessed reality that there is now a perfect synergy involving our body and His life!

Through Jesus, in whom the human and divine natures are re-joined, we can escape the corruption that spoils our humanity and share in the divine nature of God.

---

3   Paul Butler, *Theology and Life: The Study of God* (Global Ministries and Relief Inc., 2005).

ME VINE, YOU BRANCH!

In my opinion, there is no clearer picture of this incredible union between God and the new creation than when Jesus teaches it in John 15. He uses the analogy of a vine and a branch to demonstrate what our restored new creation life should look like.

> *'I am the true vine, and My Father is the vinedresser. Every branch in Me that does not bear fruit He takes away; and every branch that bears fruit He prunes, that it may bear more fruit. You are already clean because of the word which I have spoken to you. Abide in Me, and I in you. As the branch cannot bear fruit of itself, unless it abides in the vine, neither can you, unless you abide in Me. I am the vine, you are the branches. He who abides in Me, and I in him, bears much fruit; for without Me you can do nothing. If anyone does not abide in Me, he is cast out as a branch and is withered; and they gather them and throw them into the fire, and they are burned. If you abide in Me, and My words abide in you, you will ask what you desire, and it shall be done for you. By this My Father is glorified, that you bear much fruit; so you will be My disciples.*
> *John 15:1-8 (NKJV)*

Here we see Jesus helping the disciples to understand something that was potentially very difficult to grasp, by using a simple object lesson. He chose a vine and a branch to communicate what I term 'the order of our existence'. What He taught them reveals a couple of very important things that, for the sake of time and focus, I have listed below:

- He is the vine, we are branches. He does not exist because He is joined to us, but we exist because we are now joined to Him.
- He calls us to do one thing and that is to abide, or remain, in Him; to stay connected to the life that we now have because of our union with Him.
- It is when we separate ourselves from Him that we get into trouble. Then, withering and decay begin, leading to death.
- The branch does not and cannot prune itself; it trusts the gardener to do this. Also it cannot provide in itself what it needs to be healthy; rather it looks to the vine.
- When we stay joined to Him, we naturally produce the fruit He requires and we bear fruit that both remains and that glorifies Him.

If we go back to the original garden again (Eden) for a moment, for the sake of another comparison, we can witness another powerful 'reverse manoeuvre'. In Genesis we see Adam turn in his rebellion from knowing the spiritual life of the tree of life, to eating of the fruit of the forbidden tree, which was the tree of the knowledge of good and evil or, put another way, the tree of 'I know better than God, I choose to be my own

God'. When Adam ate of the tree, the nature of the tree became his nature, and suddenly sin was in the veins of humanity and unholy had become his, and our, condition. And remember, in their removal from the garden, God said that they could no longer have access to the tree of life; they could not know its (His) spiritual life or nature anymore. In essence, they are like branches that have been broken from the tree of life and become grafted into the life of the other tree, by this joining they had now become partakers and expressions of its nature.

Now picture this: in redemption it is as if, at the moment of our salvation, Jesus walks across that garden again, but this time He breaks you off from the tree you are connected to by your first birth and walks back across the garden, rejoining you, grafting you back into the tree you were originally made to know: the tree of His spiritual life. In the same way, the life of the other tree had a daily, unforced expression in you because of your union with it. Now, so it is with the tree of life. Its life becomes your life, its (His) nature is now your nature. There may well be a hole on the trunk of the tree that you were formerly a part of, where you were once positioned, but the reality is that you are not connected there anymore! The death and unrighteousness that is within its sap is no longer the sap that comes into the branch of your new life; it may still spew out of the vine, rise up the trunk and come out of the hole that was once where you were joined, but it no longer comes into you and is no longer your nature!

Now you are a partaker of His life; He did not leave you in the garden somewhere in between the two trees, but grafted you back into Himself and gave you access to His own life again. Just as the vine and branch that Jesus spoke of had a shared life, so now do we with God. The life of God (His breath and Spirit) now flows into Christ the vine and through you, the branch, because you are now one with Christ, having been placed into Him by the hand of the great gardener, God. Think about that for a moment: if you are a believer then His life is now your life, His breath is your breath! All He wants you to do is breathe, to stop panting the self-sustaining breath of a dead you and draw upon the richness of life that He has now re-joined you to know. So why not go ahead and take a moment to breathe it in deeply and let it out?

Many Christians sadly get themselves into a lot of self-effort related problems because they have a misunderstanding of this fundamental truth. Instead of acting like a branch, and daily sucking on the sap of the vine to which they are now joined, they try to produce the fruit God says He requires, but in their own ability. In their striving they sadly resemble constipated apple trees, rather than

> All He wants you to do is breathe, to stop panting the self-sustaining breath of a dead you and draw upon the richness of life that He has now re-joined you to know.

flourishing trees that produce fruit on a daily basis and that glorifies the Father. The error is that they are striving to produce the fruit, instead of yielding to the nature that produces it. Have you ever heard an apple tree straining to produce apples? No! Why? Because it's a natural thing that is the consequence of a successful union. As a branch yields to the life that is in its vine, health is constant and fruit comes naturally. All Jesus told us we need to do is abide, or remain, in Him. As we remain, His life (breath/nature) now flowing in us, will naturally produce the new fruit that He called us to bear. It's in the yielding!

Think honestly for a moment about the following questions:

- Do you know and believe that you have been broken off the old tree through your identification with His death, burial and resurrection?
- Do you believe that in Him you were born anew and came into newness of life, that you became a new creation?
- Do you believe that He has not only broken you off, but also grafted you into Himself again? That He is the vine and you are a branch?
- Do you believe that the sap (nature, Spirit and life) that is in Him, now comes into you? That you don't produce it, you yield to it as you abide in Him by faith?

These are important questions to ponder, because

what you believe to be true really is the most important thing. What you truly believe will be what causes the transformation God wants you to know. If you can agree with these simple facts then all you need to do now is breathe in and breathe out. As you do you will begin to experience, in a much greater way, His life flowing through you on a daily basis, just as a branch does. You see, the secret of our lives as believers is our union with Him.

> You see, the secret of our lives as believers is our union with Him.

> *For in Him we live and move and have our being, as also some of your own poets have said, 'For we are also His offspring.'*
> **Acts 17:28 (NKJV)**

ANOTHER RELATIONAL WAY OF LOOKING AT IT

Allow me now to go a little deeper with this thought, as we continue to consider this union with Him and the shared life we can now know because of it. We have spoken of the vine and the branch, now let's make it more relational and talk about the union between a man and a woman, so that we can see how we now have a relational union with Him.

> *Do you not know that your bodies are members of Christ himself? Shall I then take the members of*

Christ and unite them with a prostitute? Never!
Do you not know that he who unites himself with
a prostitute is one with her in body? For it is said,
'The two will become one flesh.' But whoever is
united with the Lord is one with him in spirit.
1 Corinthians 6:15-17 (NIV)

Here again we see the principle of union with God; with an opening statement, Paul brings us into the depths of this amazing reality by asking the question: 'Do you not know that your bodies are members of Christ Himself?' To be a member of something is to be a part of it; just as your arms are members of your body and enjoy the same blood and oxygen as your body, so are we now joined to Him. Paul then begins to talk about what transpires between a man and a woman when they come together sexually, and the fact that two who were once separate become one in this union of intimacy. He uses the negative example of a man and a prostitute, but the fact remains within any context of sexual relationship, that two become one. We see this reality come into being in Genesis 2:24 when it speaks of 'two becoming one flesh'. This is something instituted by God that should be kept safe within the covenant of marriage; this truth is also spoken of in the New Testament as well in both Matthew 19:5 and Ephesians 5:31. People do not realise as they should that there is a joining or coupling together that comes when they sleep with someone, and when they choose to sleep around it is not just a physical thing, but rather a joining that occurs much deeper in the lives of those involved.

Paul then uses this relational stage he has built, concerning people becoming one, to deliver the incredible truth that whoever is united, other translations say 'joined', with the Lord are one with the Lord. Again we see the principle of shared life expressed, when we join ourselves to the Lord by coming into the salvation He provided; it is not a physical thing but a spiritual one. Don't get me wrong, your physical-self will be affected by it, but it is a spiritual joining. Once again, it is at this moment that you enter back into the garden and are reconnected to the umbilical cord of His divine life. He is now joined to you and you to Him. You are now, as Paul said, one spirit with God! This is why you can now hear His voice and know His leading internally, this is why you can experience the gifts of His Spirit operating in your life and see the fruits of the Spirit spring into blossom as His nature and life flow into you activating, enabling and empowering you to please the will of the Father and to live the new-creation life that is now yours. He did not just give you a new life at salvation, but He put a new heart and new spirit in you: His Spirit! This was always His intention and was foretold clearly by the prophet Ezekiel.

Then I will sprinkle clean water on you, and you shall be clean; I will cleanse you from all your filthiness and from all your idols. I will give you a

*new heart and **put a new spirit within you;** I will take the heart of stone out of your flesh and give you a heart of flesh. **I will put My Spirit within you** and cause you to walk in My statutes, and you will keep My judgments and do them.*
Ezekiel 36:25-27 (NKJV)

This is how we experience true and lasting transformation in our lives, God working inside of us. Unlike a lot of the modern gospel messages that are based on self-achieved external change and behaviour modification, based on the ability of the person, the Spirit-filled believer yields daily to the Spirit of God and the Word of God. As they do, transformation occurs and they are transformed. They are supernaturally changed into the image and likeness of God, the same likeness we lost in the fall of Adam.

But we all, with unveiled face, beholding as in a mirror the glory of the Lord, are being transformed into the same image from glory to glory, just as by the Spirit of the Lord.
2 Corinthians 3:18 (NKJV)

Notice it says 'with unveiled face'. An unveiled face is a married face – to be married is to be one with someone else. The normal Christian life is all about you knowing that you are now in Christ and that Christ is now in you. This is what empowers us to walk as overcomers and to take hold of all that He secured for us to know and to have.

HIS BREATH (LIFE), NOT OURS

Let us consider our new birth a final time, and take one final moment to ponder the relationship and union of a child and its mother, specifically while the child is still in the womb, because this is the state that we have spiritually returned to, through coming into Christ.

> The normal Christian life is all about you knowing that you are now in Christ and that Christ in now in you.

As I've mentioned before, I have five children – four girls and one boy – and I was at the birth of each one of them. Prior to them being born there was the presence of a heartbeat; the doctors would even let me listen to it. Yet, at this point they were still in the womb of my wife and not breathing the air that we breathe for themselves. Contained in a sack of fluid they breathed, but not as we know breathing to be. This thought intrigued me, so I did some research to find out how the baby was breathing without breath, or breath as we know it.

An unborn baby doesn't breathe through their mouth or nose in the womb – that won't start happening until they're born. Babies grow in the womb filled with amniotic fuild. Their lungs are not yet fully developed, and are not used for breathing. Instead, the baby gets its oxygen, as well as all the other important things it needs to grow, through the umbilical cord that connects the baby to its mother, and through the placenta.

When a mother breathes in, all the oxygen she needs, and her baby needs, go into her body and is shared between her and the baby; and when she breathes out, all the byproduct of her body's natural processes and the baby's – mainly carbon dioxide – is expelled. The mother is breathing for the baby, and the mother's body handles the exchange of oxygen and carbon dioxide for both herself and the baby.[4]

A child in the womb relies on the mother (parent) for their total life, existence and well-being. Everything that they need comes to them through the umbilical cord that joins them to the mother. When the mother breathes, her breath becomes their breath and, within that breath and the common blood they share, is everything they need to both survive, and for the child to develop into all it is meant to be. I love the picture of this relational connection. Remember what we have been emphasising: we have been joined to God through Christ, we are now one spirit with Him, a divine umbilical cord

> We do not wait to stop breathing naturally to experience this real life, as it is ours the moment we believe, for He has placed eternity in us now.

---

4   Summarised from *How do babies breathe in the womb*, by Dr Tina St, John, https://www.livestrong.com/article/27084-babies-breathe-womb/, accessed on 11/04/18.

has been connected to us and we now draw our true life from Him. It is not mere mortal life, like we knew, but eternal life: *zoe* life. When He breathes, we breathe. His life is our life; we draw upon His breath and no longer need to depend on the self-sustaining pants of a fallen, breathless Adam.

> *I have been crucified with Christ; it is no longer I who live, but Christ lives in me; and the life which I now live in the flesh I live by faith in the Son of God, who loved me and gave Himself for me.*
> **Galatians 2:19 (NKJV)**

Eternal life means: life never ending. One day, our bodies (the last part of us to be glorified) will cease to breathe natural breath. In that day we shall not die because He is the resurrection and the life. Though our natural flesh shall stop drawing upon the oxygen that sustained it, we shall live on. How? Because our true life, which is eternal, is found in Him; a new life that we received and were joined to at our second birth – salvation. We do not wait to stop breathing naturally to experience this real life, as it is ours the moment we believe, for He has placed eternity in us now.

> *He has made everything beautiful in its time. He has also set eternity in the human heart; yet no one can fathom what God has done from beginning to end.*
> **Ecclesiastes 3:11 (NIV)**

In and through Jesus, you have been joined back to God. His *zoe* life is yours to know and enjoy right now. The Garden of Eden is open again for you, not as a physical place called Eden, but as a state of being. So why would anyone stay outside its gates, settling for mere existence?

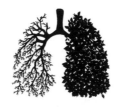

Chapter 5

EDEN NOW

*I*n the last chapter we concluded by asking the question: if Eden, as a state or condition of being and as restoration to God's *zoe* life, is available now for all who come through Jesus, why would anyone who is entitled to know it not come through the gates, fully into it? The answer, I believe, is fairly simple. It is normally because of one of two things: ignorance or unbelief!

IGNORANCE

Firstly, let us look at ignorance. If a person does not know that something is available, maybe because nobody told them it was, then they will never fully participate in what is available for them to know. Think of this naturally: if you were going to a concert and had tickets to get in, but no one told you that your ticket entitled you to special seats, as well as a backstage experience afterwards, then you would go to the show and enjoy it, but not experience and enjoy what you were fully entitled to. Though you would enjoy the experience, to some degree, you would be unknowingly settling for a lesser experience of it than you could have known. So it is with understanding the truths concerning what God has made available to you in your salvation. In Hosea 4:6 God reveals that His people perish or 'are destroyed from lack of knowledge' (NIV), from a lack of knowing what was both intended for them and available to them. It is vital that we study the Word and allow the Holy Spirit to lead us daily into greater understanding, specifically understanding concerning what is now ours, in and through Christ. God wants you to know the benefits that are now yours, it's the devil who wants to keep you in the darkness of ignorance, so that he can continue to steal from and destroy your life (John 10:10). The remedy for this is that we know His benefits and never forget them; let's take another moment to breathe and let King David remind us of some of these incredible benefits.

> *Bless the LORD, O my soul; and all that is within me, bless His holy name! Bless the LORD, O my soul, and forget not all His benefits: Who forgives all your iniquities, Who heals all your diseases, Who redeems your life from destruction, Who crowns you with loving kindness and tender mercies, Who satisfies your mouth with good things, so that your youth is renewed like the eagle's.*
> **Psalms 103:1-5 (NKJV)**

DON'T ACT LIKE A PAUPER WHEN YOU'RE A PRINCE

There really are so many great and wonderful benefits to this great salvation the Lord has given us (Hebrews 2:3). But if we are ignorant of the benefits and entitlements that are now ours, we will walk the earth settling for a lower level of life than God intended for us to know.

As it says in Ecclesiastes 10:7, we will walk the earth as paupers when we are actually princes – and that's not because He hasn't fully given everything but because we have not yet fully received it. A good Old Testament account that portrays this very well is the story of Mephibosheth, the son of Jonathan and grandson of Saul. In 2 Samuel chapter 9 we are introduced to Mephibosheth: he is a crippled young man, crippled because as a child he was dropped by the nurse who was caring for him, and he was permanently disabled because of her negligence. He lived like a beggar, making ends meet and scraping together a living. This is sad, but what is more sad is that at the same time, David the king was looking for him to bring him into a better way of living, but Mephibosheth was ignorant of this fact. It was while he was praying one day that David remembered the covenant he had made with Mephibosheth's father, Jonathan. They made a covenant that meant that Jonathan, and any of his offspring, were entitled to half of David's kingdom. This was an amazing thing, but the problem was that as David searched for Mephibosheth, with the desire to restore him, Mephibosheth hid from David out of ignorance. You see, people had told him that David was mean and only had harm in his heart towards him, so instead of being in position for his moment of inheritance, he hid himself away, afraid in the ignorance of other people's lies. In reality things couldn't possibly have been more different. You see, the truth was that David had nothing but good in his heart towards him!

Eventually, David's horsemen found Mephibosheth and, as he cowered in fear of being harmed, they picked him up and took him into David's kingdom. Then came the moment that he had dreaded: the moment when he met David. But as he watched in amazement, David seated him at his table: the chair gave him sameness of stature with the king, and the tablecloth covering the disabilities in his legs. Then he was further amazed, even dumbfounded, as David announced with great joy that Mephibosheth was entitled to half of his kingdom, and had been since his birth! There were no catches involved, because this was his birthright. What an amazing moment that was for Mephibosheth as, in one single moment of time, his life changed forever. He no longer had to be his own provider or protector; he no longer had to crawl through life as a pauper; now he would ride as a prince. No longer would he know the self-sustained life he had existed in before; he would now know the life of a king. As I mentioned before, the really sad thing about this account was that this inheritance had been

Through Christ, we have been made heirs and joint heirs to a king and His kingdom.

his for a long time – actually, from his birth he had had the right to claim the position and inheritance he now knew. Only one thing kept him from it, that one thing being ignorance! By living in the opinions and lies of others, he had lived untrue to his birthright, not finding out who he truly was and the benefits that were available to him. Now, think about this in the light of our lives and redemption; through Christ, we have been made heirs and joint heirs to a king and His kingdom.

For all who are allowing themselves to be led by the Spirit of God are sons of God. For you have not received a spirit of slavery leading again to fear [of God's judgment], but you have received the Spirit of adoption as sons [the Spirit producing sonship] by which we [joyfully] cry, 'Abba! Father!' The Spirit Himself testifies and confirms together with our spirit [assuring us] that we [believers] are children of God. **And if [we are His] children, [then we are His] heirs also: heirs of God and fellow heirs with Christ [sharing His spiritual blessing and inheritance]**, *if indeed we share in His suffering so that we may also share in His glory.*
Romans 8:14-17 (AMP, emphasis mine)

One of the benefits of being an heir with Christ is our entitlement to be partakers of God's life, to have intimate fellowship (shared life) with Him, and to know the quality of life that Adam knew in his original, pre-fallen state. If no one has told you this, you need to know! You have an entitlement and right to come back into Eden – you are accepted in the beloved (Jesus) and you belong!

It was back in 2016 that the Lord started to stir a revelation in my heart concerning this reality. He began to speak another two small words deep into my spirit man. Those two words were simply: 'Eden now'. As with 'restore' and 'breathe', I could not get these two words out of my head, and I began to meditate on them. I would pray: 'What do you mean, "Eden now"?' 'What does that mean to my life here on earth?' Initially, I began to think that He was merely reminding me of my entitlement, to know heaven one day, that I could be assured that when I died I would be in paradise with Him. That was good, don't get me wrong, but I sensed a much deeper understanding trying to break through into my own understanding. I sensed that the Lord was trying to underline something else as He released these two words over and over into my spirit.

Then, a few days later, it suddenly dawned on me what God was saying. He was revealing to me that I did not need to wait until heaven to know a state of being that was completely comparable to the state of being that Adam had known in Eden. That He had secured a one hundred per cent redemption, so that I could know it

> One of the benefits of being an heir with Christ is our entitlement to be partakers of God's life, to have intimate fellowship (shared life) with Him, and to know the quality of life that Adam knew in his original, pre-fallen state.

now! I could experience Eden: His *zoe* life, His protection and provision – here and now. Just as we don't wait until we die to receive His kingdom, but come into it and it into us here on earth the moment we believe, so it is with the restored Eden-life. It is for us to know and be partakers of here and now, not just one day in the far, far away.

THE VEIL WAS TORN IN TWO

I began to, once again, meditate on what Jesus achieved as the last Adam, and began to further unwind, or reverse, the negative things that the first Adam had produced, and consider what the ramifications were for humanity. In what I believe was a God-inspired revelation, I saw it! I saw the angel with the flaming sword, who guarded the way back to Eden, stepping aside, unblocking the way back in and making access to God's spiritual life possible again. When did this take place? Two thousand years ago, in that moment, when the veil in the temple was torn in two. You see, the veil in the temple was only in place because of what Adam had done. Adam's sin had produced the need for there to be separation between the creator God and the creation He had made, who had become corrupted. From the moment Adam was removed from Eden, there was always the need for

> The veil in the temple was only in place because of what Adam had done.

something that separated a holy God from an unholy people, unholy now because of their sin.

As we established before: God loved us too much to destroy us, but had to construct and maintain a controlled environment to allow a level of continued relationship with us. This environment and the separation were only needed until an appointed day – the day of our

> In that moment, when He breathed His last human breath, He opened up the way for us to breathe our first rejoined spiritual one.

redemption; that day being the day when Jesus went to the cross. Once again, as stated before, He went both for us and as us, and the moment He shed His precious blood, declaring, 'It is finished', the debt of sin that was on our lives was fully settled! In that moment, when He breathed His last human breath, He opened up the way for us to breathe our first rejoined spiritual one.

The Bible records that it was at that exact moment in the temple court when the curtain, or veil, separating that which was holy from that which was unholy, was torn in two. This could only mean one of two things. Either, a holy God had become unholy to be reunited with His lost creation, or, that a holy God had just made an unholy people holy, and an unrighteous people righteous again. How? By one single act of sacrifice and obedience at a cross by His one and only beloved Son. Think about this moment: the veil was torn in two, not by the hands of man, because it was far too thick to be torn by man; it could have only been torn by the hands of God, a God who wanted to remove everything that separated Him from those He had perfectly redeemed and restored.

*Now from the sixth hour until the ninth hour there was darkness over all the land. And about the ninth hour Jesus cried out with a loud voice, saying, 'Eli, Eli, lama sabachthani?' that is, 'My God, My God, why have You forsaken Me?' Some of those who stood there, when they heard that, said, 'This Man is calling for Elijah!' Immediately one of them ran and took a sponge, filled it with sour wine and put it on a reed, and offered it to Him to drink. The rest said, 'Let Him alone; let us see if Elijah will come to save Him.' And Jesus cried out again with a loud voice, and yielded up His spirit. **Then, behold, the veil of the temple was torn in two from top to bottom;** and the earth quaked, and the rocks were split, and the graves were opened; and many bodies of the saints who had fallen asleep were raised; and coming out of the graves after His resurrection, they went into the holy city and appeared to many. So when the centurion and those with him, who were guarding Jesus, saw the earthquake and the things that had happened, they feared greatly, saying, 'Truly this was the Son of God!'* **Matthew 27:45-54 (NKJV, emphasis mine)**

Some key things to note:

- God turned His back on His Son because, at that exact moment, His Son had become the sin of the world, all of it at one moment in time, on one person.

- Jesus cried out one last time and gave up His Spirit, He breathed the last breath of His natural-born life. He, and the humanity in Him, now dying, needed death to secure the promised resurrection to newness of life.

- At the exact same moment of Jesus' death, the veil that separated God from man was torn from the top to the bottom. At that same moment the earth quaked and graves burst open, the Bible records that those who were known to have died were seen walking around town. Why? Because the *zoe* life of God had left the containment of the temple, no longer needing to be segregated, God brought life to every place He passed by.

This moment is so significant to our understanding of coming back into Eden because, I believe, it was at this moment that the angel with the flaming sword we referred to previously, stepped aside. The need to keep sin away from God was now removed because those who found new life in Christ found full forgiveness of sin in His cleansing, shed blood. The issue that demanded the need for separation was now completely settled in Christ.

So, as we consider and come into agreement with the

truth of what God has done for us, in qualifying us for that which we did not deserve, we remove the ignorance that keeps us from walking in that which is ours to know. Furthermore, we find acceptance as we step, by faith, into everything He has provided for us. His Word is light (truth) and it will always dispel darkness (ignorance). That's why we must know His truth, because His truth is what sets us free and keeps us free. The truth for you today is: if you have come into Christ, the gates of Eden are wide open and beckoning you to enter, so that you can experience what it is to truly breathe His life.

UNBELIEF

Unbelief is different to ignorance and carries a very different attitude and spirit with it. With unbelief we generally know, or have heard, what God has made available for us, but we choose not to believe it, or doubt that it is true. By doing this we are actually calling God a liar, and we bring a question mark to the validity of His Word and faithfulness.

Unbelief is a very serious and disqualifying thing because it opposes the simple belief, or childlike faith, that we are called to have. Just as a child trusts the words of his parent without questioning them, so, too, God desires us, as His children, to believe every word and promise He gives us, even when they look impossible and we cannot see how He is going to do what He said He is going to do. Unbelief pridefully stands before God, declaring that we know more than Him, that His Word can't actually be fully trusted. We cannot afford to let unbelief have any rule or reign within us because every good thing that God promises us involves us believing in Him and His Word to apprehend it. When you read through the Gospels it's amazing that the one thing Jesus continually rebuked people for, especially the disciples, was concerning unbelief. Over and over again He would say things like, 'Only believe', 'Repent from your unbelief', 'Oh, you of little faith'.

Why is dealing with unbelief in our lives so important? Because, like I said, everything we get from God involves faith and everything He wants us to do for Him also must involve faith, if it is to please Him.

> *But without faith it is impossible to please Him, for he who comes to God must believe that He is, and that He is a rewarder of those who diligently seek Him.*
> *Hebrews 11:6 (NKJV)*

Faith (believing what He has said) is the most vital part of us engaging with God and His promises. Even when it pertains to our salvation, we see it's actually our faith that brings us into the glorious salvation He has provided and that joins us to this life He has invited us to know. This remains true, independent of whether you be a Jew or a Gentile, our connection to God's salvation is always a matter of faith (our believing) alone. Once again, using a tree as an analogy of being joined to Him, let's look at how Paul applies the importance of faith to our salvation in Romans 11:

> *For if the firstfruit is holy, the lump is also holy; and if the root is holy, so are the branches. And if some of the branches were broken off, and you, being a wild olive tree, were grafted in among them, and with them became a partaker of the root and fatness of the olive tree, do not boast against the branches. But if you do boast, remember that you do not support the root, but the root supports you. You will say then, 'Branches were broken off that I might be grafted in.' Well said.* **Because of unbelief they were broken off, and you stand by faith.** *Do not be haughty, but fear. For if God did not spare the natural branches, He may not spare you either. Therefore consider the goodness and severity of God: on those who fell, severity; but toward you, goodness, if you continue in His goodness. Otherwise you also will be cut off.* **And they also, if they do not continue in unbelief, will be grafted in, for God is able to graft them in again.**
> *Romans 11:16-23 (NKJV, emphasis mine)*

Here we can clearly see that being saved (joined to Him) is an issue of faith alone! It teaches us a number of key truths that are worth taking a moment to pull out:

- Holiness is the result of connection, not self-achievement. We, as branches, experience holiness because of our union to a holy root. When we understand this, we can cease from trying to be holy by external things that we do and, instead, we begin to simply live true to His holiness that is in us because of our union with Him. He has made us holy and has placed His Holy Spirit in us that makes us twice holy, a correct understanding of this will cause you to be holy because He is holy (1 Peter 1:16).

- In our salvation we were broken off from a tree that was wild by nature (sin nature) and have been grafted in to the tree of life, and can now partake (2 Peter 1:4) in the fatness of the life of its root (Romans 11:17), a root that is holy.

- There is no place left for arrogance or boasting, only faith, because we do not support Him, He supports us. Again, this truth is found in what Jesus taught in John 15:4-5.

- Independent of whether you are Gentile or Jewish by natural descent, salvation is relative to you being joined to the Vine (Jesus) by faith alone. People are added and removed independent of their natural heritage, solely according to their faith. It is by faith that we are saved (joined to Him), through His grace alone.

Knowing this, let us never under-play or under-estimate faith, and the power of us being 'believing-believers'. It is faith that brings us into right relationship with Him, faith that causes us to possess the things He promises us, and it is the simple footsteps of faith that cause us to walk back into an Eden state of living, to breathe again, so that we can know a condition of rest that He promised we could. We will now look at this promised rest more deeply, but as we leave this chapter remember: only believe! All things are possible for those who believe. So believe and breathe!

Holiness is the result of connection, not self-achievement. We, as branches, experience holiness because of our union to a holy root.

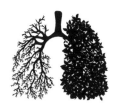

Chapter 6
ENTERING INTO HIS PROMISED REST

Now we come to what is, in many ways, the most important chapter for those desiring to experience 'Eden life' now, and desiring to breathe as God designed them to. In the previous chapters we laid a solid platform concerning what God has made available for us to know through the perfect redemption of His Son. However, I have not yet given enough guidance concerning how a person can now step into it and take hold of what we have termed 'Eden-now living'. So, this is what we will now set out to do.

Think back with me again to the two small words that the Lord spoke to me at the very beginning of this journey; they were 'restore' and 'breathe'. Remember also how we have established that before a person can experience God restore, they have to come through the first four letters of the word which are: REST. To come into a rest that God provides is actually our inheritance and the very thing that causes us to experience a brand-new way of breathing in this life. The Bible reveals that the Lord has provided a rest for you to know and to live out from, so the real question is: have you entered into this rest that He has provided for you?

Please take a moment to read the invitation that the Lord gives us to enter into His rest, I have included a larger chunk of scripture because it really needs to be read in full. Take a moment to read through these passages and discover the incredible invitation within them.

Therefore, since a promise remains of entering His rest, let us fear lest any of you seem to have come short of it. *For indeed the gospel was preached to us as well as to them; but the word which they heard did not profit them, not being mixed with faith in those who heard it.* ***For we who have believed do enter that rest***, *as He has said: 'So I swore in My wrath, "They shall not enter My rest,"' although the works were finished from the foundation of the world. For He has spoken in a certain place of the seventh day in this way: 'And God rested on the seventh day from all His works'; and again in this place: 'They shall not enter My rest.' Since therefore it remains that some must enter it, and those to whom it was first preached did not enter because of disobedience, again He designates a certain day, saying in David, 'Today,' after such a long time, as it has been said: 'Today, if you will hear His voice, do not harden your hearts. For if Joshua had given them rest, then He would not afterward have spoken of another day.* ***There remains therefore a rest for the people of God. For he who has entered His rest has himself also ceased from his works as God did from His. Let us therefore be diligent to enter that rest***, *lest anyone fall according to the same example of disobedience.* Hebrews 4:1-11 (NKJV, emphasis mine)*

Firstly, notice that twice it refers to a rest that is still available to the people of God today, in verse 1 saying 'it still stands' and in verse 9 that 'it still remains'. Then it begins to unpack the thought that this rest now being offered to us was available to other people before us also, but they did not enter into it or experience it, why? Because of two things: unbelief and disobedience. You see, the entrance into the rest that God provides for us to know really is through faith alone. As we learned in the previous chapter, faith simply being us choosing to trust and believe in what He has promised.

This rest that God offers us is not the result of, or a reward for our striving or performance. Rather it is the result of us simply believing in what He says He has made available for us to know and then the receiving of it by faith. Notice that this passage also states that those who were offered His rest before us, did not mix it or unite it with faith, so they did not ever experience or inherit it in their lives. It's good for us to remind ourselves once again that all that actually matters to God regarding our involvement in inheriting things is our faith! Will we just simply trust Him concerning the things He has made available?

But without faith it is impossible to please Him, for he who comes to God must believe that He is, and that He is a rewarder of those who diligently seek Him. ***Hebrews 11:6 (NKJV)***

So it is through faith alone that we enter into all that God provides for us, whether it be our salvation, our healing, or indeed this rest that He has made available for us to know, in this life and not just the one to come. To enter His rest, Hebrews also teaches us, that we must have ceased from our labours or efforts (verse 10) but also that we should be diligent, or strive to enter it (verse 11). What does it mean to be diligent, or strive to enter this rest? Is that statement not a contradiction? No, it's actually not! What Hebrews is saying is that we need to be attentive and persistent in our faith (believing and trusting Him) to remain in the rest He has provided for us, by His grace; to labour, to fully live in and enjoy that which cost you nothing, simply because you were invited to.

WHAT ABOUT SABBATH REST?

When reading through these verses in Hebrews 4 you will also notice that it mentions a 'Sabbath rest'. This can sometimes be confusing to some people who were raised in churches, where they were taught that Sabbath rest was relative to one day in the week, normally Sundays. They were probably taught, as I was, that it was God's plan and design that we take one day of the week as a time to refresh and replenish ourselves and to concentrate and even dedicate it to Him. My response regarding this now is simply: yes, I still believe this principle is true and that it still serves a meaningful purpose in the weekly life of the believer. However, I also believe that Sabbath rest is a bigger thing for the believer than just one day a week. I believe it is also to be an invited way of life that

his is such a rich passage of scripture that reveals so
h concerning what Jesus achieved as our High Priest.
mpares Him to the priests of the old covenant
had to continually stand and perform their duties
use their task of dealing with the sins of the people
never finished and could actually never be completed.
esus, our High Priest, it says that when He gave
life and shed His blood as our sacrifice, He completed
demands that were in place that were needed to
re and redeem us. When He had done this, He sat
n. Think about that for a moment. There are only
reasons a person sits down: either because they are
, lazy or because they have finished what they came
.

sus sat down for the latter. When He said from the

cross, 'It is finished', He

npleted work has
e our completed
and His rest is
our rest too!

meant it was *completely
and utterly* finished. After
finishing what He had
come to do, He ascended
to heaven to sit again next
to His Father. What did

ome to do? Save us! To make full payment for our
and to completely repair the damage that Adam had
ed for humanity in his act of disobedience. We need
ve a revelation that He is now seated, but also that
now seated in Him. His completed work has become
completed work, and His rest is now our rest too!

should be a part of the daily lifestyle of the believer as well.

Let me open that up a little bit further to make sure
you are correctly hearing the point I am making. I believe
that God indeed designed for man to know a 'Sabbath
day' in his week, because He knew, as our designer, that
we worked better and more productively in the six
remaining days when we rested for one day in our week.
Just as we were taught to let the fields rest every few
years to allow them to
refresh and restore, so we
would also benefit from the
same principle operating
in our lives on a weekly
basis. This one day a week
would be like a tithe to
Him, a day where we cease
from our labour to be with
Him, enjoying the benefits
of the life He blessed us
with. As I have said, I
personally still believe all of these things and still hold
true to the principle of having a day a week to rest and
replenish. This day of rest, for me as a minister, is not
often a Sunday but normally a Monday. Independent
of the day of the week that I choose, I endeavour to
remain true to why God set this in motion.

The point I really want to make is that I also believe
that experiencing the rest that He provides is a much
bigger and better deal than a one-day-a-week experience.

Sabbath rest is a bigger
thing for the believer
than just one day a
week. I believe it is also
to be an invited way of
life that should be a part
of the daily lifestyle of
the believer as well.

Rather, God wants us to know a state or condition of rest every day of the week, a rest that remains strong in every season of our life, independent of whether we are in a time of calm seas or a time of stormy ones. It is not even that we rest from physically working, or fulfilling the commitments we need to fulfil, but rather a rest from the striving and anxiety-based way of living that we once knew when we were in Adam! It is about an internal rest, a better and much healthier state of living that flows from you knowing that your life is now safe in His hands.

The fact is that in Adam there was no real rest, rather there was the toil and sweat of self-protection and self-preservation, until one day he returned to the dust (Genesis 3). In Jesus there now is a rest that God has restored for His people to know, that is based in His providence. Now that we are in Christ, we can know a promised rest in our lives that is much more than just Sunday off, and we can know His rest in regard to those things we used to strive to achieve by our efforts and performance. Things like trying to make God love us, and striving to please Him and to gain His acceptance. The truth is, we are now loved and accepted in His Son and the need for striving has ceased.

> *To the praise of the glory of His grace, by which **He made us accepted in the Beloved.***
> *Ephesians 1:6 (NKJV, emphasis mine)*

You see, this rest that we now know in Him, as I have

said, is not so much a rest from physi and taking care of daily commitmer the inner strivings we knew before w It is when we understand that He co we know that *we* no longer need to t is not until we know where He finish know where we are to begin.

Remember what it says in Het cease from our labour as He has cease we know what He finished and fulfi it causes a rest within us concerning our responsibility to achieve ourse positioned to live in that which He longer to spend our lives trying to do has already done and created for us.

HE SAT DOWN AND SO DID WI

The Bible says that after completi be done, He sat down!

> *Day after day every priest stands ar religious duties; again and again he sacrifices, which can never take awa this priest had offered for all time o sins, **he sat down** at the right hand since that time he waits for his ene his footstool. For by one sacrifice he perfect forever those who are being*
> *Hebrews 10:11-14 (NIV, emphasis m*

But God, who is rich in mercy, because of His great love with which He loved us, even when we were dead in trespasses, made us alive together with Christ (by grace you have been saved), **and raised us up together, and made us sit together in the heavenly places in Christ Jesus,** *that in the ages to come He might show the exceeding riches of His grace in His kindness toward us in Christ Jesus. For by grace you have been saved through faith, and that not of yourselves; it is the gift of God, not of works, lest anyone should boast.*
Ephesians 2:4-9 (NKJV, emphasis mine)

Remember what we have been saying over and over again: when we were saved God took us out of Adam and placed us in His Son; we are now in Christ and seated in the Lord's completed work. This means that we no longer need to daily try to achieve the things that have been achieved and settled for us by Him; rather, we can rest in His victory.

This seems so simple but so many believers actually don't do it. Rather, they live in a constant state of inner exhaustion and strife because they are trying to achieve or maintain something that has actually already been completed and finished. The Bible calls this 'dead works'.

CALLED FOR GOOD WORKS NOT DEAD ONES

The Bible speaks of good works and dead works. Good works are what come from our lives because we know

123

we are saved, they are the natural fruits that grow from the branches of the tree that is connected and yielded to the life of the vine. Dead works are very different; they are what believers do in ignorance when they try to gain what they already possess. For example, it would be like a bald man trying to shave his head: it is a pointless activity because he is already bald. Or, imagine a person trying to put a plug in the sink when there is already one in there. Again, it is a pointless work or a dead work because what they are trying to do has already been successfully done by someone else.

If you want to enjoy this rest that God has given you to enjoy, then it is vital that you understand what He has completed for you in His death, burial and resurrection.

So it is for the person who is constantly trying to save themselves by the things they do; it is a waste of time and is totally unneeded because such activity was the requirement of the law under an old covenant (agreement between God and man), where now, Jesus has brought us into a new and living covenant by the shedding of His blood which has fulfilled the requirements of the law regarding what was required by us, and has left us in a place that we are seated in a completed salvation, in Him. Our salvation is not based upon what we can achieve, but rather on what he achieved for us; He has perfected us by His blood. So now He

124

invites us to live in the rest of His finished work, not strive to make it happen. If you want to enjoy this rest that God has given you to enjoy, then it is vital that you understand what He has completed for you in His death, burial and resurrection, otherwise you will spend your life doing dead works to achieve something you already possess. Always remember that you are a new covenant (agreement) person, a covenant based only on what He achieved for you.

By calling this covenant "new", he has made the first one obsolete; and what is obsolete and outdated will soon disappear.
Hebrews 8:13 (NIV)

I remember once hearing a story that paints this truth really well. It spoke of an old man who was going to do some carpentry. He was getting ready to saw some wood and looked for his favourite pencil. Not finding it, he became agitated and started to think about where he had last seen it. Eventually, totally annoyed, he emptied his shed of all its contents and, having still not found it, got busy putting everything back into his shed, spending the best part of a day to do so. Frustrated, he stood in the garden still trying to remember when he last saw it. Just then, his wife appeared and asked why he was looking so upset? He explained how he had misplaced his pencil. Then, with a smile on her face, she revealed to him: it was behind his ear. The whole time he was looking for his pencil, he already had it but was ignorant of it, so had just wasted his time.

Many people sadly do this consciously or subconsciously regarding their salvation! They constantly do things to earn it or sustain it, rather than living in the finished inheritance of it. Take a moment now to stop and consider what He has completed for you in regard to your salvation and then take a deep breath and BREATHE. God wants you to now grow in Him from the place He has positioned you to know and no longer try to produce it.

RESTING IN HIS LOVE

There are also other areas in our life and Christian experience that we can find ourselves striving instead of resting. One area being our understanding of His love for us. Just as you cannot earn your salvation by what you do, you can't earn His love by what you do either. Remember, He loved you before you gave Him a single thought. He loved you when you were still lost in your sins, why would He love you any less now? As we are raised in this life, we can sadly sometimes experience a love that needs to be earned from certain people. When we act a certain way they love us, and their love can be very dependent on or related to our ongoing performance. God's love is not like that, it is Agape love: a love that flows from a mind and heart that is settled – settled on loving us. Because we live in a world where love so often needs to be earned, we can sometimes bring that way of thinking and loving into our relationship with God and, before long, we are trying to achieve, earn or maintain His love as we have with other people's love.

Let me say again, some people do this consciously, others subconsciously but either way it is an inner striving that can determine not just your perception of God, but also what you feel you need to do to qualify your life to deserve or warrant His love. Once again, simple truth can end this striving and bring us back to a healthy state of breathing if we will allow it. The truth is that He loved us while we were sinners; His love for us is not dependent on our love for Him or our performance.

Allow me to remind you of some verses that underline this essential truth:

But God demonstrates his own love for us in this:
while we were still sinners, Christ died for us.
Romans 5:8 (NIV)

But God, who is rich in mercy, because of His great
love with which He loved us, even when we were
dead in trespasses, made us alive together with
Christ (by grace you have been saved).
Ephesians 2:4-5 (NKJV)

See what great love the Father has lavished on us,
that we should be called children of God! And that
is what we are!
1 John 3:1 (NIV)

His love cannot be earned, we may demonstrate our love for Him by what we do (John 14:15) but His love for us is eternally settled and was demonstrated in Him giving His only beloved Son to save and restore us so now we should simply rest in His love or, put another way, enter into the rest of His love, by faith.

> *He brought me to the banqueting house, and his banner over me was love.*
> **Song of Songs 2:4 (NKJV)**

RESTING IN HIS PROMISES

The final area I want to address regarding ceasing from our striving and living in His rest is in regard to God's promises. So often, when people are believing God for something and are standing on a promise God has given them regarding it, instead of resting in the promise they labour to try and make what God has said He would do happen – often, actually, even trying to help God to do it. I believe when it comes to the promises of God we need to remember this simple truth: if God wants your help, He will ask! So often it is when we try to help God to do what He promised He will do, that we mess everything up, ruin things and burn ourselves out. God never actually asked you to do that, did He? He asked you to believe, that's all.

That sounds so easy, but just like our father of faith, Abraham, sometimes we just can't help ourselves and we start trying to help God, but all we do is create an

Ishmael that has to be managed instead of enjoying the Isaac that God promised He would bring to pass. Am I saying you need to be lazy? No, I am saying you need to learn to rest in the armchair of faith when it comes to the promises of God, that your striving will add nothing to what God is doing; in fact it can seriously get in His way. Considering Abraham again, think about the account of God promising Abraham and Sarah a child: everything looked impossible to this childless couple, then God turns up in the midst of this impossibility and says, 'I am going to give you the child you desire.' What did God expect them to do? Absolutely nothing! Just to believe and watch Him do good on what He promised He was going to do, but they just had to get involved and a plan was hatched between them involving Abraham sleeping with another woman and producing a child that was to cause serious ramifications that last even to today.

> I believe when it comes to the promises of God we need to remember this simple truth: if God wants your help, He will ask!

So let me simplify how God wanted it to play out. Abraham was to receive the promise, then he was to go and sleep with his wife (faith without works or natural corresponding actions of agreement being dead), then they were meant to just recline in the armchair of faith knowing that God is faithful to His Word and what seemed impossible would come to pass because He is both the author and finisher of our faith (Hebrews 12:2). What He authors, He finishes. Time and time again in the Bible we see God operate in accordance to this principle: people believed His promise and inherited what He promised them they would. So it is too for us today: God wants us to know the rest or armchair of faith regarding His promises. He wants us to be diligent to hear and receive His promises by faith and then to rest in the promise knowing that He is the author and finisher of what He has said yes and amen to; this is not just for little promises, but the massive ones too.

We need to move from a type of faith that seeks to help God out into the rest of faith that says: 'I am going to sit in the armchair of believing God will do what He said He would and I will see Him bring to pass what He promised.' For some of you today that are in the middle of a very real situation, where you have been believing in God for what seems to be the longest time, this is exactly what you need to hear. God does not want you to strive but to find rest in His promise. He doesn't want you hyperventilating as you try to work out the how, when and who; rather He wants you to lean back and breathe deep, knowing that He will do good on what He promised He would do. Remember, if He needs your help, He knows where you live and will ask! If He does not ask, then just relax and breathe because He is the one who is going to make the way where there seems to be no way.

So, whether it be in regard to our salvation, His love, or things we are believing for based on the promises He has given us, we need to live in a place of rest that comes through faith, not strife that is the fruit of ignorance or unbelief.

You need to be personally persuaded concerning:

- What He has finished for you.
- What He has promised He will do for you.
- That He is the author and the finisher of the things He has promised.

Stop and take a moment to check your heart regarding these three specific things: are you striving, performing or resting? Take a moment to breathe: if you have His Word and His promise, you have Him, because He is His Word and His promise!

REMAIN SEATED IN THE RIGHT CHAIR

A good friend of mine once put it this way. He said: 'There are three chairs available for us to sit in, and they all begin with the letter 's': Separation, Salvation and Self-effort.'

When we are saved He takes us from the chair of separation and seats us in the seat of salvation. It's in the seat of salvation that we have everything we ever need, from this chair we are meant to live in a condition of rest. But sadly it's not long after being saved that we can shift our lives from being seated in the chair of salvation into the chair of self-effort. We start to labour and try to make things happen rather than simply trusting in God for all we need and all He said He would do. It is in this seat of self-effort we become exhausted and frustrated, but what are we to do? Simple, we move back to the middle seat of salvation where we know again what it is to be in Him and to where we know Him taking responsibility for our lives. We are never to go back to the seat of separation, but neither is it our destiny to be seated in the chair of self-effort. Being seated in Him is our inheritance, an inheritance that gives us promised rest.

WE ALWAYS START WHERE HE FINISHED

Think once again about Adam in chapter one of Genesis. Adam's first day was God's last day! Notice that God made everything on His own, by Himself (between the triune being of who He is), and when He was happy it was as it should be He then made man and positioned him in His finished work. So when Adam opened His eyes and breathed His first breath he experienced what God had finished, not what he had to now help God finish. So it is with those who have been born again. With and through His only beloved Son Jesus and by His Spirit,

Father God did everything that was needed to justify and redeem man, to remove the sin that had disqualified us and to make all things that needed to be, renewed.

When Jesus said from the cross, 'It is finished', He meant it. Everything that was needed to be done to restore us and bring us into His rest was now successfully in place and just as with Adam in creation, we do absolutely nothing to help Him make it happen and can add nothing to it! All we do is enter into His finished work, by faith.

When a person is born again they awake in a new place that was created for them by the work or labour of another. Just as they did not make this new place by their effort so they can't sustain this place by their efforts they are simply called to enjoy it and remain in it by faith.

> The truth for you and for me is that we are at our best when we live from rest!

Adam's deep breathing in the garden flowed solely from his union with God and a simple childlike faith that left him trusting in the providence of the one who had made him to protect him and provide for his every need. So it is also for us now: it is not a fairy-tale; we really can know an anxiety-free way of breathing as we understand our lives have been restored to a state of being called: 'Eden Now'. So thanks be to God, Sabbath rest for us is no longer just one day a week, but our destiny and our intended lifestyle.

This rest, you see, is our inheritance in Christ and

God wants each of us to enjoy it and to remain in it. Sometimes it is easy for a person to find this rest for a moment but much harder for them to remain in it; they come into it but then come straight back out of it into what they believe to be normal life. The truth is that God does not want you to experience it at random moments in your life, so that you can be refreshed momentarily, He wants you to live in it and live from it so you don't grow weary and in need of rest. The truth for you and for me is that we are at our best when we live from rest!

To be honest with you, in my experience it is often remaining in His rest that can be the more difficult part, because so many things in our daily lives seem to want to grab us and pull us out of His rest back into the crazy life and condition of living we formally knew in Adam. We have to be deliberately conscious, or 'labour diligently' to remain in the rest He has given us and refuse to leave 'Eden life' and go back to knowing the mere existence we once knew before. Eden must become our new home, our state of being. We have found in Christ a far superior way of breathing, let us not exchange this any more for the shallow breathing of Adam. You may

> Eden must become our new home, our state of being. We have found in Christ a far superior way of breathing, let us not exchange this any more for the shallow breathing of Adam.

have spent your life unknowingly popping into Eden then popping back out – this needs to stop. It is now time for you to learn to remain in His rest. When life is busy and when it is not, when the oceans of life are calm and when there are storms blowing strong all around you. You see, the rest He provides is not subject to what is going on outside of us but rather what is happening deep within us. Remember, John 15 did not say, 'visit the vine for top-ups every now and then', it said that we are to abide and remain in the vine.

WAKING UP IN REST

When the Lord first started to speak to me about this, I asked Him to show me the areas in my life that I was not living correctly in His rest. I was amazed when He began to show me the areas we spoke of earlier, namely the completeness of my salvation, His settled love for me, and the promises He had given me. If you would have asked me if these were settled or if I was in rest regarding them, I would have certainly said yes. The truth was: I was in my rest, not His. Without knowing it, when I woke up in the morning, somewhere on the inside of me there was still an element of who I was that was in many ways unknowingly still trying to earn or qualify my salvation by the things I did, and still trying to make Him love me by the things I did and did not do. I would get out of bed and instead of sitting in the armchair of faith, begin to 'help God' fulfil the things He had promised He would do for me. He wanted all of this dead work activity to stop!

But it is sometimes hard to change long-term habits, isn't it? But this is what we have to do if we want to live in His rest.

After finding His rest in a new and powerful way I purposed in my heart that I was no longer going to pop in and out of it. One of the ways I started to re-educate my inner habits that would cause me to strive rather than rest was I made the decision to settle these three things I struggled with before I even got out of bed. What did this look like? Well, I invented a new habit: when I woke up in the morning, before I did anything else, I laid there and established some truth in my thinking. I would pray: 'Lord, before I get up I am going to purpose to remain in your rest.' Then I would declare: 'I am saved and nothing I can do today can add to it, I only need to live from it! Thank You that today I am lavishly loved, my performance or lack of performance changes nothing. Your love for me is a settled thing that comes from You and is not produced by me, today Lord I will live in Your love. And regarding all the promises You have given me and my family. Lord, if You need me to do anything show me, but until You do I am going to sit in the armchair of faith knowing You will finish what You have promised. Amen.'

Then I would get out of bed, but get out of bed in rest! I actually did this for many weeks until it became a habit and I still return to doing it every time I feel my rest being disturbed and inner strivings reappearing. If you struggle with remaining in His rest maybe pray the prayer I did every morning, or write one that is more bespoke to you and the things that disturb His rest in your life.

So, we are no longer called to strive but rather to live an anxiety-free life where panic attacks and hyperventilation are no longer our daily norms but rather a deep breathing that contains His peace that passes all understanding. Remember once again the invitation of Jesus to you.

> *Come to me, all you who are weary and burdened,*
> ***and I will give you rest***. *Take my yoke upon you*
> *and learn from me, for I am gentle and humble in*
> *heart, and you will find rest for your souls. For my*
> *yoke is easy and my burden is light.*
> *Matthew 11:28-30 (NIV, emphasis mine)*

This was not a random statement but rather it runs directly alongside other statements He and Paul made regarding knowing a worry-free life and a different way of living to what we have known before. The good news is: there remains a rest for the people of God. So, enter it today and purpose to remain in it; as you do you will discover the life and breathing patterns He intended and indeed gave His life for you to know.

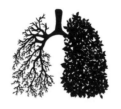

Chapter 7

THE CAREFREE LIFE

an this really be true? Does God really want us to know a care-free and worry-free life? These are good questions but the real question is: do you think He would have said these following words if they were not actually true, if these promises were not actually available?

*Therefore I tell you, **do not worry** about your life, what you will eat or drink; or about your body, what you will wear. Is not life more than food, and the body more than clothes? Look at the birds of the air; they do not sow or reap or store away in barns, and yet your heavenly Father feeds them. Are you not much more valuable than they? Can any one of you by worrying add a single hour to your life? And **why do you worry** about clothes? See how the flowers of the field grow. They do not labor or spin. Yet I tell you that not even Solomon in all his splendor was dressed like one of these. If that is how God clothes the grass of the field, which is here today and tomorrow is thrown into the fire, will he not much more clothe you—you of little faith? **So do not worry,** saying, 'What shall we eat?' or 'What shall we drink?' or 'What shall we wear?' For the pagans run after all these things, and your heavenly Father knows that you need them. But seek first his kingdom and his righteousness, and all these things will be given to you as well. Therefore*

do not worry *about tomorrow, for tomorrow will worry about itself. Each day has enough trouble of its own.*
Matthew 6:25-34 (NIV)

Was He exaggerating? Or was the Son of God genuinely welcoming people like us to know a whole new way of living and breathing that was based upon, and solely dependent on, faith (believing Him)?

When reading these verses you can't help but notice how many times Jesus instructs the reader 'do not worry', but why would He say the same thing so many times in one conversation? We know Him not to be someone who wasted words or used them lightly. So was He offering a fake deal that sounded great in theory but wasn't actually real? No! Absolutely not! What He was offering them then, and us today, was real! He was offering a new way of living, a pace of living that would not take your breath away with fear, anxiety and panic rather let you experience and partake in His own *zoe* life. He came so that we would know it (experience it for ourselves), not just know about it!

I came that they may have and enjoy life, and have it in abundance [to the full, till it overflows].
John 10:10 (AMP)

Allow me to remind you again that the original word that is used for life here is not the word normally used for the everyday life that we know because of our first birth (*bios*), rather God's own life (*zoe*), the same quality of life that God enjoys He has now made available to us, our true inheritance being to have fellowship (enjoy sharing life) with Him. Another wonderful truth worth grasping is that the Lord also invited us to cast all of our cares (anxieties, fears and stresses) on Him and in doing this we are not being weak or acting irresponsibly, rather we are choosing to come into and experience the protection and provision that He now invites us to know.

> He is saying to us, 'Cast your cares on Me because I am now responsible for taking care of you!'

In 1 Peter 5:7 it says that we are to cast all our cares and anxieties on Him, because He cares for us. This is such an incredible invitation, but the reality is that you will only truly cast your cares and anxieties away when you know someone else is taking responsibility for them, and that is exactly what God is saying here. He is saying to us, 'Cast your cares on Me because I am now responsible for taking care of you!' It is when we get a revelation of this amazing truth and begin to relax into it that we truly begin to live from the promised rest He has given us to enjoy.

DECLARING YOUR DEPENDENCE

The good news, or should I say great news, is that we can now know a carefree life because we are, as Adam originally was, again dependent on Him. You see, when Adam (man) sinned he claimed or initiated a state of independence from God. Independence is a very interesting subject, especially for Americans. Every July 4th, America celebrates something known as 'Independence Day', but what does this day refer to? What are Americans actually celebrating? In case you don't know, July 4th is when America celebrates, as a nation, the day that they became autonomous (self-governing), the day they left the covering and the sovereign rule of England, the nation that had originally established them. In planning their future America chose independence rather than to continue to be ruled over or governed by someone else, and in signing the Declaration of Independence on July 4th, 1776 (although apparently it was actually August 2nd!) they became responsible for themselves as a nation. By claiming independence, they were now fully in charge of and responsible for themselves.

Without wanting to over compare what the leaders of America did to what Adam did, it remains a great example for us to be able to paint a picture of exactly what Adam did when he (as A.W. Tozer termed it) 'committed high treason'. Adam's single act of rebellion and disobedience caused him to have to leave the covering of God that was all he had ever known. He became autonomous or self-governing, and in doing this he took his well-being and future, as well as that of the human race, into his own hands.

We can now know something very different because

when we are born again in Christ we experience, as I termed it before, another 'reverse manoeuvre'. By this I mean that in that very moment of us being born again, we turn from the state of independence we inherited in Adam back into a state of total dependence that has been renewed and sealed for us by Jesus. This is life-changing truth that declares once again that everything for us changes the moment we believe! In that moment, we repent of our sin (our independence) and return to His covering and government; His care and providence (provision and protection) become renewed in and over our lives, and we can once again enjoy the fruits and rewards of a life that is again dependent on Him. A life that lives free from, and above, the anxieties and fears that those who don't know Him, or are not submitted to Him, are still very much subject to. A life where we can breathe deep again, knowing our lives and indeed all of our days are now in the hands of, and under the control and care of, a loving protective heavenly Father.

The Apostle Paul also echoes these thoughts regarding the carefree life in his letter to the Philippians:

Be anxious for nothing, but in everything by prayer and supplication, with thanksgiving, let your requests be made known to God; and the peace of God, which surpasses all understanding, will guard your hearts and minds through Christ Jesus.
Philippians 4:6-7 (NKJV)

Or, as *The Message* translation more colourfully puts it:

Don't fret or worry. Instead of worrying, pray. Let petitions and praises shape your worries into prayers, letting God know your concerns. Before you know it, a sense of God's wholeness, everything coming together for good, will come and settle you down. It's wonderful what happens when Christ displaces worry at the center of your life.

So those who have been redeemed are to now daily cast their cares on Him and enjoy the peace that He provides, a peace that displaces the worry and anxiety that once ruled within their unredeemed hearts and lives. Instead of worrying, we enter the rest that is now ours and diligently purpose to remain in it, no longer worrying or striving to produce things that are promised and eternally finalised, rather enjoying the benefits of all that is now completed.

THE CAREFREE LIFE IS A HEALTHY LIFE

The truth is that anxiety and worry are not God's will for your life! Peace of mind and a state of inner health and well-being are. Anxiety is a strategy of the enemy for your life and is really not good for you, as it affects and damages your life and well-being far beyond just what happens in your thought life. Any doctor will tell you that anxiety, fear and worry can not only fill your mind and heart with dread but they can also cause extremely negative ramifications in a whole lot of other areas, from your appetite to your health, and even affecting your relationships. It has been medically proven that anxiety in a person's heart can cause a whole lot of other things in their life that affect a person physically, mentally and emotionally. Things like fatigue, headaches, muscle pain and tension, nausea, breathing problems, suppression in the immune system, digestive disorders, memory loss, artery disease, heart attacks, depression and addictions to different things can all be attributed to this thing called anxiety. So don't for a moment underestimate the effect it can have on your life.

The medical world tries its best to provide or recommend cures and management programmes for these things, most of which are not wrong but often never deal fully with the root that is the cause. Things like healthy eating, regular exercise, counselling or therapy, relaxation methods and CBT all have an effect and can help, but I believe God offers something much better and more effective: He offers us a worry-free life! A solution that does not just deal with the current fruit and gives you relief for a moment but rather deals with the root and exchanges an unsustainable peace for a sustainable one as He takes the reins of responsibility again to the life He has given you to live.

Cast your cares on the Lord and he will sustain you; he will never let the righteous be shaken.
Psalm 55:22 (NIV)

Pile your troubles on GOD's shoulders—he'll carry your load, he'll help you out. He'll never let good people topple into ruin.
Psalm 55:22 (MSG)

HE'S GOT YOUR BACK

God wants to trade your anxieties and fears for His peace and rest! The success of this trade will always come down to being a matter of faith, to you trusting another who invites you to trust Him! It must involve you not just trusting Him for the things you can see, working out the outcome with your own reasoning, but also the things that you cannot see and have no idea how they could ever work themselves out for good. God wants you to trust that He has got your back covered regarding the seen things and the unseen things (Deuteronomy 29:29). You can know His rest in stormy times; when others around you are freaking out you can be enjoying peaceful slumber. Just like Jesus did in the boat when the disciples were running around screaming 'we are gonna die', you can know a rest that comes from a deep persuasion within you that God is in control. Just as the servant of Elisha had to discover, when it looked like his cabin was surrounded by the enemy, that God had it covered for Him, so He does for us. Let us take a moment to remind ourselves and encourage our hearts with this account of God at work behind the scenes in this account with Elisha and his servant.

When the servant of the man of God got up and

*went out early the next morning, an army with
horses and chariots had surrounded the city. 'Oh
no, my lord! What shall we do?' the servant asked.
'Don't be afraid,' the prophet answered. 'Those
who are with us are more than those who are with
them.' And Elisha prayed, 'Open his eyes, LORD, so
that he may see.' Then the LORD opened the
servant's eyes, and he looked and saw the hills full
of horses and chariots of fire all around Elisha.*
2 Kings 6:15-17 (NIV)

The account starts with the prophet and his servant
asleep in a cabin. Elisha the prophet had infuriated the
King of Aram because he kept prophetically revealing
to the King of Israel his plans, which had caused him one
defeat after another. So the King of Aram sent his army
to Dothan, where Elisha was, to capture him. Unaware
that their cabin was totally surrounded by the enemy,
Elisha's servant woke up, and on the way to the bathroom
he took a casual look out of the window. To his shock
and horror he saw the enemy army surrounding them,
so he ran to the prophet and woke him up – just like the
disciples did to Jesus when He slept in the boat. He woke
him up saying, 'Oh no, my lord! What shall we do?' I
personally think this is the translator of the scripture
adding an element of respectability to the moment, and
the servant was probably more realistically running
around the cabin screaming something like, 'Wake up,
we are going to die!' Or perhaps, 'Why are you sleeping?

We are about to be slaughtered!' Something more along those lines.

The prophet just turned over and kept on sleeping. Eventually, because of the screams of his servant, he got up and looked out of the window and seemingly without taking much notice of the enemy army simply said to his servant, 'Don't worry about it.' Then he qualifies this statement by saying, 'There are more with us than with them.' The servant still could not believe this because what he could see out of the window, with his natural eyes, defied it. So the prophet, now out of bed, goes to his servant and prays for him, praying a simple prayer, 'Open his eyes, Lord, let him see what is really happening right now.' Suddenly, the servant looked out of the same window he had before and still sees the same enemy army he had seen before, but now he saw another army that surrounded them. He saw the hills filled with the Armies of God, golden chariots and horses, and every anxiety within him suddenly ceased. The Army of God did not come when the prophet prayed, it had been there all along – that is why the prophet slept and enjoyed a state of rest while the servant was screaming his head off. You see, the prophet knew he was in God's hands and God had his back. He did not need to worry because his God was working behind the scenes for his protection and his good.

HE'S ALWAYS AT WORK BEHIND THE SCENES

We need to realise this, too, that now we are back in

'Eden living', we can live a carefree life even in what would naturally seem like stormy times. We can sleep while others are freaking out because we know that God is taking care of us, because we have cast our cares on Him. He is now working in all things for our good!

> *In the same way, the Spirit helps us in our weakness. We do not know what we ought to pray for, but the Spirit himself intercedes for us through wordless groans. And he who searches our hearts knows the mind of the Spirit, because the Spirit intercedes for God's people in accordance with the will of God.* **And we know that in all things God works for the good of those who love him, who have been called according to his purpose.**
> *Romans 8:26-28 (NIV, emphasis mine)*

Did you read that? *All* things, not some things! As we commit to love Him and walk according to His calling and Kingdom purposes, He takes care of the rest. Again you enter into the rest of this truth by believing that He will do what He promised. I have preached this verse many times over the last twenty-five years of ministry. Normally when preaching it I say, 'God works behind the scenes

> We can sleep while others are freaking out because we know that God is taking care of us, because we have cast our cares on Him.

for those who love Him.' It really is just like a play at a theatre. We love to look at the actors on the stage for Act I, but we rarely ever notice or pay any attention to the shadows of the people moving behind the scenes who are getting things ready for Act II. When it comes to pantomimes or classic fairy stories, nothing ever looks good or right at the half-time interval. Normally, half-way through the performance the baddies are winning, the good people are slaves or servants and everything looks like it is going wrong. Then in the final Act everything suddenly changes, the good people win and the bad people lose, and everything ends 'happily ever after'.

But what if you left the theatre at half-time? You would not witness what had been happening behind the scenes that would turn the story around for good. Listen, if you are going through something right now the key is: don't leave the theatre or give up! Don't let anxiety, that is based in fear, take your breath away. Rather, lift your eyes to the one who promised He would take care of you and trust that what He is doing in the unseen of this moment is for your good. He has your back like He promised He would. As I heard it sung recently in a worship song we have been using in church: it may look like you're surrounded but you're surrounded by Him.

When you read the account in the book of Esther of how she overthrows Haman, it really is just like a theatre show with two halves. You have the 'goodies' – Esther and her uncle Mordecai – and you have the 'baddy' –

Haman, who wants to kill Mordecai and the whole Jewish nation. You see Haman desperately working behind the scenes for the harm of Mordecai, even building gallows for him to hang on – but God had a plan! The moment Haman went backstage to do harm to God's people, God went backstage to turn it for their good! The moment Haman got involved in sneaky plans that would create holes for Mordecai to fall into, God was busy making bridges that he would walk over. Haman built a moment of destruction for Mordecai, but on the night it all went terribly wrong and Haman ended up hanging on the gallows that he had made for Mordecai. The Jewish nation were saved and given favour, Mordecai also took over Haman's job. It is just like a theatre show, right? The unseen star was God, He was the one working in the unseen for the good of those who trusted in Him, and He will do the same for you. All He wants you to do is trust Him, to walk by faith in His promises, not by sight or any other natural sense that you received in your first birth.

He calls us to simply cast our cares and anxieties on Him and, as we do, we live in what He provided for us to know – a carefree life. Be anxious for nothing, for 'no thing'! Breathe deep, knowing that He takes care of what has been committed to Him. Jesus knew His Father doing this throughout His earthly ministry. Whenever His enemies set up moments of destruction for Him He always walked away from them unharmed because His time had not yet come. The Father always had His back and no weapon that was being fashioned against Him could prosper. Even in the darkest moments before His death. Look at what He prayed to His Father before He entered into the unprecedented moment of dying and going to the belly of hell, to take back the keys that Adam and Eve had lost.

> *It was now about noon, and darkness came over the whole land until three in the afternoon, for the sun stopped shining. And the curtain of the temple was torn in two. Jesus called out with a loud voice, 'Father, into your hands I commit my spirit.' When he had said this, he breathed his last.*
> **Luke 23:44-46 (NIV)**

Jesus was voicing the prophetic words of David found in Psalm 31:

> *Into your hands I commend my spirit; you will redeem me, LORD, God of truth.*
> **Psalm 31:5 (NABRE)**

He was totally confident that in whatever lay ahead of Him over those next couple of days, as He gave up His natural breath to redeem us, He was safe because He had committed His life and mission to God and He knew, as Paul said so well in 2 Timothy 1:12, God was well able to keep that which He had committed to Him.

As the sky turned grey and the sun stopped shining,

He stood on the edge of something that no other man would ever face, a darkness no man could ever conceive in their wildest dreams. Then, He stepped boldly into it, knowing His Father could be trusted to redeem Him. How about you? Will you trust that same Father to keep what you commit to Him? He invites you to! It's when you do that you truly find His rest,

> Will you trust that same Father to keep what you commit to Him? He invites you to!

because if His hands are on it then yours no longer need to be. Trust Him, He is faithful.

A PRAYER FOR YOU

Father, I pray for the reader that You would help them to cast on You everything that may be weighing them down or causing fear within them. I pray that as they cast their cares on You that they would know the promised peace that passes all understanding bring rest to the innermost unseen parts of who they are. Even in the midst of real storms that may be currently raging they would know the peace of being in Your hand and hear You speaking to the storms 'peace be still'. Amen.

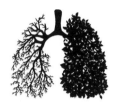

Chapter 8

GOD'S BREATH
BRINGS LIFE

*M*y prayer and hope at this point of our journey together is that your breathing has been seriously affected and your life blessed by the truths we have journeyed through together. Also that you are experiencing a change of pace and new rhythms of life deep within you, as you breathe His breath with Him.

Whenever we see a reference to God's breath in scripture it is most commonly regarding the giving of life or the restoring of life to a person or a thing. We have been referencing this reality a lot within the ruling context of this book. We have seen how, in the beginning, God the Father breathed into man's nostrils and he received His life and Spirit and became a living being. We also need to consider another very powerful account of God breathing His life into man that is found in the New Testament, an account that massively affects us and is very relevant to us as New Testament believers. I am speaking about the incredible moment when we see Jesus the Son, in the moments before He ascended, do the very same to His disciples that God the Father did to Adam in Genesis. What a truly incredible parallel this is:

> *Again Jesus said, 'Peace be with you! As the Father has sent me, I am sending you.' And with that he breathed on them and said, 'Receive the Holy Spirit.*
> **John 20:21-22 (NIV)**

At this point the Lord Jesus had now risen from the grave, sin had been dealt with and death defeated. In these moments before He was to ascend back to the Father to be seated at His right hand, He came and did something very significant: He breathed on His disciples. Notice that

He did not just pray for them in a traditional way, rather He breathed on them, saying, 'Receive the Holy Spirit.'

He did not just pray for them in a traditional way, rather He breathed on them, saying, 'Receive the Holy Spirit.' The word for 'Spirit' here is the Greek word *pneuma* which, according to Strong's concordance, means: *'the third person of the triune God, the Holy Spirit, coequal, coeternal with the Father and the Son'* and *'a life-giving spirit'*.[5] Just as it had happened for the first man Adam in the garden at creation, these men received God's *zoe* life (Holy Spirit) and were then sent out. Sent out to do what? Sent out, now infused with His breath, to bring others back to life, true life, *pneuma*, the *zoe* life of God. The good news for us is that throughout the ages, this has remained the same. So, when we received 'the Spirit' we did not receive a modern one that had a slight resemblance to the original, but the very same Spirit these men received that day He breathed on them, the very same breathe that Adam received in the garden. That

5   James Strong, *Strong's Exhaustive Concordance of the Bible*, (Hendrickson Publishers, Inc., 2007), G4151.

is why we can confidently declare today that we, too, are Spirit-filled!

NO LONGER MERE MEN!

When you understand that God has now placed His breath (Spirit) in you and that your life now hosts His Spirit, everything changes! This is the moment we are meant to cast off the chains related to the sentence of mere existence that we received in Adam and begin to run free in the new life we have received. Sadly there are many Christians who have no revelation of this truth and are still making confessions like 'Hey, don't blame me, I'm only human after all.' If God was to respond to this confession in the light of all He has now provided, He would say, 'No you are really not!', knowing all that changed when He breathed on you and deposited His Spirit in You. It was the thought of only being human that was the deception that empowered the Corinthian church to carry on accommodating sinful behaviour which was contrary to the lives that God had called them to live. When Paul came through Corinth and saw their condition, did he overlook what they were doing? No, he addressed it! He did not address it in the light of who they used to be, but in the light of who they now were. Also, we see that he did not place an emphasis on the fruit that they were producing, rather on the confusion they were living under, concerning who they now were and the ignorance that was fuelling what they were producing. Listen to how he addressed them when he arrived and discovered them living no different to unbelievers and indeed in some areas of their lives, worse than unbelievers.

> *And I, brethren, could not speak to you as to spiritual people but as to carnal, as to babes in Christ. I fed you with milk and not with solid food; for until now you were not able to receive it, and even now you are still not able; for you are still carnal. For where there are envy, strife, and divisions among you,* **are you not carnal and behaving like mere men***?*
> *1 Corinthians 3:1-3 (NKJV, emphasis mine)*

Paul had arrived with the desire to teach them some meaty truths, but found them still childlike in their beliefs and behaviour. So he accused them of behaving like 'mere men'. If there was no alternative available, Paul would have been fairly unrighteous and judgmental in doing this, but you see there was an alternative, and his knowledge that there was fuelled his directness. A few moments later, in the very same conversation he was having with them, he revealed to them this alternative, revealing who they really were.

> **Do you not know that you are the temple of God and that the Spirit of God dwells in you***?*
> *If anyone defiles the temple of God, God will destroy him. For the temple of God is holy, which*

temple you are.
1 Corinthians 3:16-17 (NKJV, emphasis mine)

Paul repeats this again a little later to the same people in chapter 6.

Do you not know that your bodies are temples of the Holy Spirit, who is in you, *whom you have received from God? You are not your own; you were bought at a price. Therefore honor God with your bodies.*
1 Corinthians 6:19-20 (NIV, emphasis mine)

In stating these things, we see Paul adamantly disagree with the identity they were settling for: an identity of being 'merely human'. This deception fuelled their belief that they were actually no different to what they were before receiving Christ. Very bluntly, we see Paul declare to them, 'You are no longer mere men, you are temples of God, God's Spirit (*pneuma*) now lives in you!' It was an awakening to this truth that would both change their behaviour and the things that they were tolerating in their lives. It would be the revelation of this very present reality that would cause the fruit of envy, strife and immorality to finally stop being produced in their lives, and allow for new fruit that pleased God to begin to spring forth, and it is this understanding that does the very same for us!

WE WERE NOT LEFT HELPLESS

Contrary to some gospels out there, God did not just save us and then tell us to make it to heaven the best we could in our own ability and strength. Rather, He gloriously saved us and then deposited His own Spirit in us to enable and empower us to live the victorious overcoming life that He said we could. His Spirit was not just given to regenerate us in our salvation but also to transform and empower us as He remains not just with us, but also in us, in this life. Remember, Jesus taught that He would not just be with us in some external experience but deep within us personally as well.

*And I will pray the Father, and He will give you another Helper, that He may abide with you forever—the Spirit of truth, whom the world cannot receive, because it neither sees Him nor knows Him; but you know Him, **for He dwells with you and will be in you.** I will not leave you orphans; I will come to you.*
John 14:16-18 (NKJV, emphasis mine)

You can see from the above verses that the plan of God was never to leave us helpless, unprotected or unassisted like vulnerable orphans, rather to come and dwell inside of us by His Spirit. He promised He would come (pour out His Spirit), and He did! After Jesus ascended and sat down next to the Father, the very next thing we see the triune God do was send the third part of the Godhead to the earth, to live not in buildings made by men but now in the hearts of men. The day of God living in temples made of brick and cement are well and truly over – now His temples are to be the lives of His followers, including you and me!

It is vital that the 'full Gospel' we claim to preach is indeed full, and includes the truth of the coming of and indwelling of the Spirit. Otherwise we will never actually break the sentence of mere existence in a person's life, as God fully intended. Rather, we offer people a new vehicle (life), but no ability to drive it any differently than before. Imagine if you knew someone who, every time they got in a car, they crashed it. Every time they got a new one they went ahead and crashed that one too. Would you lend them your car? So what's the actual problem? Is it the car or the driver? Obviously it's not the car; the problem is the driver and what needs to happen to stop cars being crashed is for the driver to move out of the driving seat and for a new driver to take control of the car and show them how to drive. This example is a great parallel concerning what God needed to do for us: we are the ones who were knowingly or unknowingly always crashing our lives; what we needed was not just 'new lives' but a new driver. Otherwise we would just end up crashing the new car (life) like the one we had before. God has provided this new driver by giving us His Spirit, His presence in our lives now causes a different experience for our lives.

Though I never set out to make this book to be

specifically about the subject of being Spirit-filled, it is actually impossible not to touch on the subject as this new breath which we are speaking of, that is now in us because we are now in Christ, is in fact the Spirit of God. Think about how incredible that is: God's Spirit is now in you!

> *But we have this treasure in earthen vessels, that the*
> *excellence of the power may be of God and not of us.*
> ***2 Corinthians 4:7 (NKJV)***

As well as teaching, guiding and helping you, as Jesus promised He would, He is in you to provide all the ability, strength and wisdom you will ever need to live out the new creation life God has given you. Whether it be strength for resisting a certain temptation in your life or the ability to forgive someone that you honestly feel is unforgivable, He is everything you now need.

THE FELLOWSHIP OF THE SPIRIT

Just as we are called to know fellowship (sharing of life) with the Father and the Son (1 John 1:3), we are also called to know fellowship (shared life) with the Spirit. Listen to how Paul ends his second letter to the Corinthian church:

> *May the grace of the Lord Jesus Christ, and the love of*
> *God, and the fellowship of the Holy Spirit be with you all.*
> ***2 Corinthians 13:14 (NIV)***

Most of us who have been around church for any amount of time have heard that statement at the end of a meeting we have been in, but have we grasped the depth of the content in that closing greeting?

We are invited to know and experience fellowship with the Father, Son and the Holy Spirit, and our fellowship (sharing of life) with the Spirit is not meant to be merely at a meeting or conference we attend but rather in the daily lives we live. We are to include Him now in everything, ask His wisdom in everything and be led by Him in everything. It is when we do this that we can say as Paul did: 'I can do all things through Christ who strengthens me' (Philippians 4:13, NKJV) and 'when I am weak, then I am strong' (2 Corinthians 12:10, NKJV). Paul was not being arrogant or boasting in his own ability, rather that of the Holy Spirit within him. He was saying, 'When I come to the end of what I have and my ability, I find Him and His.'

> Our fellowship (sharing of life) with the Spirit is not meant to be merely at a meeting or conference we attend but rather in the daily lives we live.

God never planned for us to live by our own strength any longer, it was not sufficient before so how will it be sufficient now? No, He invites us now to live in the power of His Spirit that is resident within us, no longer to do things in our strength alone but to lean and depend on Him. Did you ever notice what Jesus said to His disciples after commissioning them to 'Go into the world and change it'. He said they were to wait until they had received the Spirit. Why did He ask them to wait? Because they were still mere men, living in their own ability, and that could never change the world like Jesus intended! It was not until after Pentecost that the Lord released them to go because now, you see, they had fellowship – a sharing of life – with the Spirit and could know the power and leading of the Spirit wherever they went.

> God never planned for us to live by our own strength any longer, it was not sufficient before so how will it be sufficient now? No, He invites us now to live in the power of His Spirit that is resident within us

Sadly, some teach that the things of the Spirit were only for the original first disciples and not for us today. I cannot hold to this belief – that, I think, is just based on people putting personal experience above what's true – because when I read my Bible I see that God still calls us to be witnesses and to change the world, as He did the first disciples. Why would He not give us what we need to fulfil the common commission, like He did them? The truth is that Jesus has made available to us everything that was available to them and indeed what was available to Him when He walked the earth as the Son of Man, not just the Son of God. He had a human nature and a divine nature and had the Holy Spirit to draw upon whenever He needed! Listen, He has not short changed us or asked us to live like He modelled we should, without giving us everything we need to do so; that would not be fair or just.

No, He has made available to us today everything we need to live the life that He demonstrated for us to live. So let's be thankful that today we, too, have the fellowship of the Spirit, because the Spirit now lives in us.

You, however, are not in the realm of the flesh but are in the realm of the Spirit, if indeed the Spirit of God lives in you. And if anyone does not have the Spirit of Christ, they do not belong to Christ.
Romans 8:9 (NIV)

And you also were included in Christ when you heard the message of truth, the gospel of your salvation. When you believed, you were marked in him with a seal, the promised Holy Spirit.
Ephesians 1:13 (NIV)

*And do not be drunk with wine, in which is dissipation; but be filled (**be being filled**) with the Spirit.*
Ephesians 5:18 (NKJV, emphasis mine)

So, make sure you are drawing daily on His Spirit now within you and not being like the believers we read about in Corinth who, in their ignorance concerning what God had made available, settled for living like 'mere men'. The glorious truth is that there is no longer anything 'mere' about you! You are a supernatural person, because someone who is more super than natural lives in you and makes everything that heaven has now available to you. God's plan concerning us was not just about our justification but also our sanctification and glorification. He justified us (made us right with Himself) to sanctify us (make us clean, separated for His purposes and able to contain His Spirit) so that He could glorify Himself through us, and the lives we now live (Romans 8:30).

> He has made available to us today everything we need to live the life that He demonstrated for us to live.

This is again so relevant to living in rest and experiencing the rest that God wants us to know in our lives, that we spoke about in chapter 6. It is when we purpose in our hearts to depend on the Spirit that we truly experience the rest He promised. By depending on Him we find that we are no longer depending on ourselves, and this brings a great rest to our lives. Whether it be small hills or great mountains that need to be moved, it is great to be able to say with surety, as Zechariah did, 'Oh it's not by my might or by my power or my ability but by His Spirit' (Zechariah 4:6).

There are other times that we read about God's breath

in scripture, sometimes it appears in very noticeable ways and other times more subtly, but whenever it is mentioned, it carries great significance for the persons or things receiving or experiencing it.

DRY BONES LIVE AGAIN

When we think of God's breath in scripture it is not long before most of us think back to the prophetic moment involving Ezekiel and the prophetic vision he received from God concerning dry bones coming back to life. Let's look at this again together to see the significance of God's breath in what He was communicating to Ezekiel in that vision.

> The glorious truth is that there is no longer anything 'mere' about you! You are a supernatural person, because someone who is more super than natural lives in you and makes everything that heaven has now available to you.

The hand of the LORD was on me, and he brought me out by the Spirit of the LORD and set me in the middle of a valley; it was full of bones. He led me to and fro among them, and I saw a great many bones on the floor of the valley, bones that were very dry. He asked me, 'Son of man, can these bones live?' I said, 'Sovereign LORD, you alone know.' Then he said to me, 'Prophesy to these bones

and say to them, "Dry bones, hear the word of the
Lord! This is what the Sovereign Lord says to
these bones: ***I will make breath enter you, and***
you will come to life*. I will attach tendons to you*
and make flesh come upon you and cover you with
skin; ***I will put breath in you, and you will***
come to life*. Then you will know that I am the*
Lord.'" So I prophesied as I was commanded. And
as I was prophesying, there was a noise, a rattling
sound, and the bones came together, bone to bone.
I looked, and tendons and flesh appeared on them
and skin covered them, but there was no breath in
them. Then he said to me, 'Prophesy to the breath;
prophesy, son of man, and say to it, "This is what
the Sovereign Lord says: ***Come, breath, from the***
four winds and breathe into these slain, that
they may live*."' So I prophesied as he commanded*
me, and breath entered them; they came to life and
stood up on their feet—a vast army.
Ezekiel 37:1-10 (NIV, emphasis mine)

Three times in this account it says that God's breath
would come and when it did it would bring life and
revival, because whenever God's breath is present, life
flows. God took Ezekiel to a place, prophetically, that
looked like a valley filled with dry or dead bones. This
represents things that had once lived, once had ability,
future and hope but now were spent, slain and dead.
Scattered lifeless on the floor, they had no future or

further purpose. The Lord then asked Ezekiel a tricky question: 'Can what you're seeing live again?' Ezekiel's response was genius, in my opinion. He flipped it straight back onto God by responding 'You alone know, Lord.' What a great non-committal, keep-you-from-getting-it-wrong response by Ezekiel!

Then God said, 'Ezekiel, speak My Word to the bones, tell them that My breath is coming and when it arrives the death-like state will end and life will flow again.' Ezekiel did what the Lord told him and spoke to the dry bones that filled the valley floor. Suddenly, he heard a rattling and he watched as bones began to rejoin themselves, tendons and flesh began to appear, both joining the bones and covering them. Then God told him to speak once again, and call on His breath once more. As the prophet was obedient, he watched as those who had once been defeated and slain by enemies awoke from death, failure and loss and became restored and ready again for battle, no longer with their own life but with His. The end result was a picture that could not have been more different to what the prophet had seen at the beginning of this prophetic journey. No longer was there a valley with bones everywhere, disjointed and dead, now there was a valley filled with an exceedingly great army, standing on its

> If you are in a situation that feels like something is dead or dying, don't stay silent – start to speak.

feet and ready for battle.

This is the degree to which God's breath (life) can change things. His breath (life and Spirit) can make broken things work perfectly again, sick things become completely healed and dead things come back to life. Whether it be a physical sickness that you are battling, a relational breakdown or any other circumstance that looks, at this moment in time, like a valley full of hopeless dead bones. Like the prophet Ezekiel, you too can call on the breath of God to make things live again. If you are in a situation that feels like something is dead or dying, don't stay silent – start to speak. Don't speak mere human words that contain no real strength, but speak His Word because His Word contains life and brings life.

Notice the emphasis God placed on speaking His Word to dead bones in the account we just read: He was not just speaking, but prophesying. You see, man's words declare what is seen and obvious to the onlooker but God's prophetic words speak of things unseen and not yet witnessed. His words call things that are not as if they are.

> *(As it is written, 'I have made you a father of many nations') in the presence of Him whom he believed— God, who gives life to the dead and calls those things which do not exist as though they did.*
> **Romans 4:17 (NKJV)**

The words that God asks us to speak over death-like situations very rarely fit with what we are physically seeing or experiencing. The question is: do you want to bring God down to agree with the dead things you are experiencing, or do you want to lift those dead things up to come into alignment with what God says they can be like? Again, whether it be physical, marital or even financial, you can prophesy life, you can speak God's Word of a better day over the bones and they can live again. As He teaches us, life and death are truly in the power of the tongue, in the words we choose to speak (Proverbs 18:21). Don't stay silent; break the silence and start speaking again to dead or seemingly impossible, unmendable things, words of God's life and future. Remember not to speak your words, mere words that originate from your reasoning, but speak His Word because where the Word of the King is there is power (Ecclesiastes 8:4) and He watches over it to make it happen. Remember what He spoke to Jeremiah when he was doubting the power of God's Word coming from his mouth: 'I am watching to see that my word is fulfilled' (Jeremiah 1:12, NIV), or as He promised the prophet Isaiah:

So shall My word be that goes forth from My mouth; it shall not return to Me void, but it shall accomplish what I please, and it shall prosper in the thing for which I sent it.
Isaiah 55:11 (NKJV)

175

DO YOU HAVE A PROBLEM WITH HIS BREATH?

God's words contain life because His breath (His Spirit and life) is encapsulated within them, consider now this verse:

All Scripture is God-breathed and is useful for teaching, rebuking, correcting and training in righteousness.
2 Timothy 3:16 (NIV)

Did you see it? All Scripture is what? It is God-breathed! Not just the words that He spoke in person, to people like Moses and Abraham, but also the words that are recorded and contained within your Bible. Sadly, so many modern-day Christians need a greater revelation that the Bible is not a normal book, it is a supernatural one. The words and promises contained within it are God-breathed and contain His Spirit and His power. When a believer adds their faith to His Word, an activation takes place that lifts the Word from being written text in a book to being a powerful force in the situation that they are standing on it for. If we truly understood the power of God's Word in our hearts and on our lips, we would be making dead

> The Bible is not a normal book, it is a supernatural one. The words and promises contained within it are God-breathed and contain His Spirit and His power.

things live instead of constantly setting up home in the valley with lifeless bones.

Another great question is: does God's breath offend you? Because it is actually sometimes meant to! What did 2 Timothy 3:16 teach us that God's Word is good for? It is good for teaching, rebuking, correcting and training, not just encouragement. Too many believers only want to read the bits in the Bible that encourage them or make them feel loved, warm and fuzzy. Yet Paul teaches us that all scripture does us good, not just the bits we like. We need to get hungry again for God's breath (word) to offend us more. In His correction, rebuke and training there is also great life. It is often not until you allow His Word to offend something in your life that you suddenly find the pathway to a new way of life in that area. So don't just read your Bible in the morning, praying 'say something nice to me Lord', but get some gumption and also pray 'give me a good roasting, Lord'. I love it when He gives me a good roasting because, though it makes me sore for a moment, it always releases life and power, or as His Word puts it so well: 'Weeping may endure for a night but joy comes in the morning.' (Psalm 30:5, NKJV).

> Another great question is: does God's breath offend you? Because it is actually sometimes meant to!

HIS WORD MAKES DEAD THINGS LIVE AND BARREN THINGS BECOME FRUITFUL!

We have considered the valley of dry bones but also let us again consider the barren state of the father of faith, Abraham and his wife Sarah. In Genesis we are introduced to them as Abram and Sarai. They are blessed of God but experiencing barrenness in an area of their life, the ability to conceive a child. God steps into this storyline and promises Abram and his barren wife Sarai a child. Let's take a moment to look at this account to glean some revelation from it.

When Abram was ninety-nine years old, the LORD appeared to Abram and said to him, 'I am Almighty God; walk before Me and be blameless. And I will make My covenant between Me and you, and will multiply you exceedingly.' Then Abram fell on his face, and God talked with him, saying: 'As for Me, behold, My covenant is with you, and you shall be a father of many nations. No longer shall your name be called Abram, but your name shall be Abraham; for I have made you a father of many nations. I will make you exceedingly fruitful; and I will make nations of you, and kings shall come from you . . . Then God said to Abraham, 'As for Sarai your wife, you shall not call her name Sarai, but Sarah shall be her name. And I will bless her and also give you a son by her; then I will bless her, and she shall be a mother of nations; kings of

peoples shall be from her.'
Genesis 17:1-6, 15-16 (NKJV)

Notice that God promises Abram and Sarai the seemingly impossible, that now in the later part of their lives, with years of barrenness behind them, God arrives and promises them descendants from their own bodies. Notice that the very next thing God does is change their names. Why? Because in their names were their identity, as well as their prophetic future. In the culture they lived in a name was very significant, people were known by the meaning of the name and not just the name itself, as we do today in the west. Before God released a miracle of restoration and new life into their world He first changed their confession of themselves.

God changed Abram's name which meant 'high father' to Abraham, which meant 'father of a multitude' and his wife's name from Sarai, which meant 'my princess,' to Sarah, which meant 'mother of nations'. So, from this point on every time they introduced themselves they introduced themselves as Mr 'Father of multitudes' and Mrs 'Mother of nations', yet bear in mind that at this point they still had no children. How bizarre this must have seemed to those meeting them, when they enquired how many children they actually had.

When God changed their name, He changed their future. When He added 'ha' to his name and 'ah' to hers, He added His breath into their destiny. It was His breath that contained His life, which made the barren able to have a child. It was the words or letters He spoke into their identity that changed their identity, both naturally and spiritually, as Abraham then became the father of faith and not just of a natural nation.

God wants to add His 'ha' and 'ah' to your confession. He wants you to stop declaring things as they were, or you think they can be and to begin to declare His Word concerning the matter at hand. As you replace your former words and confessions with the ones that He gives you to speak, you too will see things revived and come back into life and the order they should be in. So don't stay silent! Read His Word, absorb His Word, speak His Word, because His Words contain His life and His ability today as they did way back then. Bring your confession and your declarations into alignment with what He is saying, no matter how crazy it seems to your mind or how opposite it is to what you are currently dealing with.

> Read His Word, absorb His Word, speak His Word, because His Words contain His life and His ability today as they did way back then.

Let the weak say, 'I am strong.'
Joel 3:10 (NKJV)

But what does it say? 'The word is near you; it is in your mouth and in your heart,' that is, the message

concerning faith that we proclaim: if you declare with your mouth, 'Jesus is Lord,' and believe in your heart that God raised him from the dead, you will be saved. For it is with your heart that you believe and are justified, and it is with your mouth that you profess your faith and are saved.
Romans 10:8-10 (NIV)

Here we have the timeless simple recipe of faith. When the Word of God is in your heart regarding something and also on your lips, there is a spiritual reaction that occurs which causes impossible things to happen. Sometimes believers can have a confusion within themselves that causes a blockage to them experiencing the things God says they can have. Some believe in their heart, yet don't speak what they believe. Others speak a whole lot, but don't actually believe in their heart the things they are declaring. Neither of these will see miracles released like they could. Scripture tells us to do both – to believe in our hearts what God has said He will do and is able to do, but then let that belief also be on our lips and in our confession concerning the things we speak or decree. Think about it, this is the very same recipe the father of faith, Abraham, used, wasn't it? He believed what God said even when it seemed impossible; He then changed His confession and brought his identity into alignment with God's revealed intent and from this simple alignment between heart belief and mouth confession, impossible things became very possible.

This is still how God wants us to walk with Him today in the twenty-first century. The passage in Romans that we read said that if we do this, regarding our salvation, then we will be saved, and will not be put to shame. Think about that: how hard, even impossible, was it for us to be saved? Yet God did it and we entered into the fullness of it through faith alone. What else that seems impossible to us, can God do if we will just exchange our dead words and confessions for His words that carry His life and potential? My friends, this is not just theory to me; Gina and I have seen so many impossible situations supernaturally turned around and miracles happen when we decided to agree with what God was saying. If we told you some of them you would be truly amazed. Let me say it one more time, whatever you are currently experiencing, stop speaking words that come from your own understanding or reasoning, based on what you feel or sense, find His promise for the situation and speak

> Whatever you are currently experiencing, stop speaking words that come from your own understanding or reasoning, based on what you feel or sense, find His promise for the situation and speak it until you believe it in your heart and then speak it because you do!

it until you believe it in your heart and then speak it because you do! It is then that you can, as we mentioned in the previous chapter, relax into the armchair of faith knowing that God will do good on what He said He would do. Knowing that He will not allow His Word to return void because His words are Spirit and life. What do you need to then do? Just breathe!

The Spirit gives life; the flesh counts for nothing. The words I have spoken to you—they are full of the Spirit and life.
John 6:63 (NIV)

My earthly life clings to the dust; revive and refresh me (give me life) according to Your word.
Psalm 119:25 (AMP)

A PRAYER OF RESPONSE

Father, forgive me for not speaking Your life-giving Word enough over things in my life that seemed dead, impossible or irreversible. I believe that Your life and power are contained in Your Words and as I exchange my words for Your Words, I too can see dry bones become a mighty army and barren things come to life and bear fruit. Thank You that today I make the decision to take greater responsibility for the things I say. Your Words are power and they are life and I am going to speak Your Words over the situations I face, no longer my own. Thank You,

Father, that today where the word of a king is, there is power and the Word of the King is in my heart and on my lips. Amen.

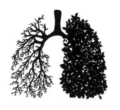

Chapter 9

MANAGING THE TRIUNE YOU

So, we have finally arrived together at the last chapter. To be honest with you, this next chapter was very nearly the chapter I left out! After finishing the previous one I initially felt I had completed the mandate of the book, but the more I thought and prayed about it, the more I felt driven to include this last one, which is much more holistic in its approach than the previous ones. Yet I honestly believe this one is also very necessary when we consider the overall well-being of you as a person. Forgive me if this last chapter sounds a little more like 'self help' compared to the chapters that have preceded it, but please hang on in there because I honestly believe it will complete our journey together in a perfect way for you. The more practical things that we will look at a little later in this chapter also contain the power to enhance and reset your breathing patterns and the pace of your daily life.

SPIRITUALLY NATURAL AND NATURALLY SPIRITUAL

Over the last eight chapters we have spoken a lot about the spiritual aspects of breathing correctly in our lives now. Specifically, how we find our correct way of breathing in Him when we come alive again to His life through new birth. When His spiritual life has been correctly plugged back into our lives, I believe it should cause both a greater state of rest and a healthier way of living in both the physical and soul-related parts of who we are.

We now recognise and celebrate that the rivers of living water that Jesus spoke about in John 7:38-39 are flowing out of the innermost being (spirit) of who we are and that these living waters (breath of God) also have an effect and bring health and well-being to the other two thirds of us, namely our soul and our body. God is not unaware of our need for well-being in the other two thirds of who He made us to be. He always intended for what He is doing through our regenerated spirit not to be isolated in its effect to the realm of our spirit-life alone, but for the flowing of His river of life now within us to powerfully and positively impact our soul and our body because they also play key parts in making us who we are.

Look how Paul highlights the effect that our spirit can have on our physical bodies:

> *And if anyone does not have the Spirit of Christ, they do not belong to Christ. But if Christ is in you, then even though your body is subject to death because of sin, the Spirit gives life because of righteousness.* ***And if the Spirit of him who raised Jesus from the dead is living in you, he who raised Christ from the dead will also give life to your mortal bodies because of his Spirit who lives in you.*** *Romans 8:9-11 (NIV, emphasis mine)*

Paul teaches very plainly here that the Spirit of God

now living in us will cause our mortal bodies to experience God-life! This is so powerful because it desectionalises some of the myths concerning the relationship between the three parts of who we are and enables us to see that our body and soul are indeed positively affected by the residency of His Spirit now alive in ours.

So it is actually biblical for us to acknowledge that the things that God does in the spirit of who we are have a positive effect on the other two thirds. The principle that health and prosperity in one part of who you are affects other parts is also mentioned by John in his third letter when his prayer for God's people was, 'I pray that you may prosper in all things and be in health, just as your soul prospers' (3 John 2, NKJV). John highlights, in this verse, that experiencing prosperity in our health can be related to the well-being or prosperity of our soul, and as we will now consider further, true well-being in our soul is related to its connection and submission to our Spirit that is now alive to Him.

> Can the things we do, or disciplines we have in the other two thirds of what makes us who we are assist or limit the effect of what God wants to do through His Spirit in our lives?

But my real question for you is this: does this also work the other way around? Can the things we do, or disciplines we have in the other two thirds of what makes us who we are assist or limit the effect of what God wants to do through His Spirit in our lives? I believe that they do. Just as in the same way the things that happen spiritually in us have an effect on us physically. It can also be true or relevant to some degree the other way around. When we stop for a moment to look at our lives in this more holistic way, we see that we are indeed, as the Bible teaches, like God, in that we are also triune in existence (three parts) made up of spirit, soul and body; the correct order of this now being we are spirit, we have a soul and we live in a body. It is good for us to understand that all three parts of us are important to God and it is His will that we experience the benefits of His breath (life) in all three parts of the person He created us to be.

When there is a correct order and alignment between these three parts that make us who we are, it can indeed cause a supernatural harmony in the complete person of who we were made to be.

Equally, when there is the presence of warring or contention between these three parts, it causes an inner conflict that produces unrest and a needless inner unsettling. So, what is the answer for this? It is simple: to create, maintain and protect a correct godly alignment and leadership order among the three parts of who we now are. As we read God's Word, we see that correct alignment from God's point of view places our alive and regenerated spirit (that is one with His) now in full charge of our life.

Firstly, we must realise this and then secondly, we are

to bring the soul of who we are – which includes things like our emotions, feelings and natural desires – under the authority and influence of the spirit. Our body is merely the vehicle that carries us around and physically enables us to carry out the desires of whoever is in charge out of the other two parts within us (soul or spirit).

As previously mentioned, before we experience new birth, we were all led by and subject to the control (leadership) of our un-renewed soul, which daily simply fulfilled the desires of our human nature, independent of whether they were good or they were not so good. When we are born again and God's Spirit comes to live in our spirit, we are then to bring our soul under the rule and reign of our spirit. As we do this our lives are then daily led by His Spirit and a new (transformed) way of living (breathing) comes into existence from deep down within us. A new way of living that now lives to please the Father, gives us a life worth living and that is a blessing to others.

Thinking this way also helps us to better define the roles of what we refer to as the human nature and divine nature in our lives.

As we said before, just as Jesus was when He was on the earth, so we now are, having no longer just a human nature within us but also a divine nature. Also, like Jesus, we too have the Holy Spirit's ability to now draw upon in our daily lives to live the lives He has called us to live. When our human nature is under the control or rule of our spirit, all is well and as it should be; it's when the human nature of a person is not under the Spirit's influence that the Bible refers to it negatively as 'the flesh', which then produces what we know as the 'works of the flesh'. When the Bible mentions the flesh in this way it is not talking about our skin or body but rather the deeds of a person that are being led by a human nature that is not under the control or influence of the spirit, or has its mind set on the things of God. Instead it is just living for its own desires and pleasure, just as it did before new birth, and in doing so it suppresses the working of the Holy Spirit and His life instead of being transformed and led by Him. Let's go back to Romans 8 to see Paul teach us further concerning this:

Those who live according to the flesh have their minds [souls] set on what the flesh desires; but those who live in accordance with the Spirit have their minds set on what the Spirit desires. The mind governed by the flesh is death, but the mind [soul] governed by the Spirit is life and peace. The mind [soul] governed by the flesh is hostile to God; it does not submit to God's law, nor can it do so. Those who are in the realm of the flesh cannot please God. You, however, are not in the realm of the flesh but are in the realm of the Spirit, if indeed the Spirit of God lives in you.
Romans 8:5-9 (NIV)

We see here that the mind or soul of a person needs to now be under the influence and leadership of the Spirit within them, which carries the divine nature and will of God. It should no longer be ruled or influenced by a human nature that is exempt of the authority or government of the Spirit. By saying this we are simply recognising, hopefully without any confusion, that now as new creation people, His Spirit is the boss in our life, and our soul and indeed human nature are now subject to and led by Him. It is when this is out of correct alignment that as Paul said we can then be 'led by the flesh' and a person defaults to fulfilling the desires of the human nature, with all of its old, natural cravings and self-established entitlements. Instead of living to please the Father, we live to please ourselves.

When this inner leadership alignment is correct, we are then as Romans said 'led by the Spirit'. When we understand these potential internal authority issues clearly, we can then submit to them being aligned as God calls them to be, and it is then that we experience the Spirit's life, well-being and supernatural peace (rivers of living water), affecting all three parts of who we are.

For me, the key is simply not to forget that your soul or your human nature is no longer the boss or driver in your life – your spirit and His divine nature are! Does our soul always like this reality? The answer to that is: certainly not! However, we should no longer give it any choice. Our spirit, that is now one spirit with His, is to be the governing and leading voice in our life throughout our life. I often teach on this important reality by comparing it to the setting of an office and what happens when there is a changing of top-level management in that office. Imagine with me that a man has been in charge of an office for forty-plus years and without warning one day there is a corporate takeover and the company he works for is bought out by a bigger and better company.

> Our spirit, that is now one spirit with His, is to be the governing and leading voice in our life throughout our life.

That afternoon the new owner of the company walks in, introduces himself and then announces that there are going to be some staffing changes; the key one being that a brand-new manager is starting with immediate effect. Then, looking directly at the previous manager, he casually says, 'Oh, and as for you, you're no longer in charge . . . *he* is,' pointing at the new guy. 'Whatever he tells you to do, you must now do it.' Having known enough managers in my life, I can't imagine for a moment that the manager who was being suddenly repositioned would just sit down and smile at what is happening. The truth is, he would probably have a lot to say, maybe something along the lines of 'Excuse me? Don't you know I have been in charge here for forty years?' To which the owner may well respond, 'Yes, that is true, and look at the state of the company and where you have not taken it.' The reality is that, independent of how the former manager may feel, from that moment on the new guy is in charge, because the owner of the company has said so, and the best thing the previous manager can do because he has not been fired and still has an important part in the company is bring his management under the leadership of the new boss.

So it is with us. There was a day when we experienced a 'corporate takeover' and it was brutal! God brought His manager, 'His Spirit', into the office of our lives and we are now to bring the former manager, 'our soul', under His governing and leadership. When we do this we experience harmony in the office (our life) and our lives go in new directions that are always so much better and much more productive than the ones the former manager took us in.

It is important that we understand that God does not hate our soul, nor does He have a desire to sack it, but He does want it to come under the rule of His Spirit now in us. Sadly, many Christians never settle this inner-management dilemma and so they remain in a state of leadership contention or limbo within themselves. This will never cause them to experience the peace or *zoe* life that God intends for them to. Everything God does always involves having correct authority in place, including what He does in us and through us. We are to now set our minds and hearts on Him and His ways and no longer be led by the self-inspired desires and leadings we formally knew. Our inspiration and guidance, now that we are in Christ, is more heavenly than earthly.

If then you were raised with Christ, seek those things which are above, where Christ is, sitting at the right hand of God. Set your mind on things above, not on things on the earth. For you died, and your life is hidden with Christ in God.
Colossians 3:1-3 (NKJV)

TAKING CARE OF THE OTHER TWO THIRDS OF US

Let's now look at how we can do some real practical things in, what we could term, the more natural two thirds of who we are, that will assist what God has done and is doing in and through the supernatural section. They are real simple, everyday things that we can do in the seen parts of who we are, that will assist and run in alignment with the things occurring or flowing in the unseen parts. Below we see Paul recognised the natural and the spiritual existences, again relating them to the two Adams.

It is sown a natural body, it is raised a spiritual body. If there is a natural body, there is also a spiritual body. So it is written: 'The first man Adam became a living being'; the last Adam, a life-giving spirit. The spiritual did not come first, but the natural, and after that the spiritual. The first man was of the dust of the earth; the second man is of heaven.
1 Corinthians 15:44-47 (NIV)

When looking at this verse in the light of what we have been saying, we see that there is a physical you that is the result of your first birth and there is a spiritual you that came into being at your second birth. The spiritual of who you are is now taking the lead of your life, but certain things that you do with the natural parts of who you are can certainly assist or work alongside the spiritual to create a complete well-being throughout your life. So in this final section let us look at seven everyday, practical things that affect us all – things that, if managed well in a person's natural life, will assist the flowing of God in their spiritual one.

Another important realisation to have as we enter this final section, which is foundational to our life, is that God wants you to enjoy this life, not just endure it! If His plan was about heaven alone then He would have killed you when you were saved, right? His Word says He gives us freely all things to enjoy (1 Timothy 6:17) and gives us all the things we need for life and godliness (2 Peter 1:3). It also says that He desires that you prosper in all things and be in health, even as your soul prospers (3 John 2). The reality is that God can do a whole lot, deep inside of the spiritual part of who you are, but if you don't manage and take care of what happens outside of you then you may not ever fully experience or enjoy it as you could. Maybe you feel like there has been a 'hole in your bucket', that you seem to be leaking out what God has been doing in you rather than retaining it as you should? Well, the chances are that it could, well be one or more of the next seven things that is causing the leak! If any of them challenge you, make the decision to 'fix the hole' so you can begin to consistently hold on to what He is doing in you. So here are seven things we all need to check the health of every now and then.

SEVEN THINGS IN OUR LIVES TO MANAGE

1) HEALTHY MARGINS

Let me ask you a simple question that I have asked myself on a regular basis. Are you continually living on the edge of the page?

You see, so many people unknowingly do; they live life without any margins in their life. When it comes to writing and reading, most would understand the purpose of margins. Why do we use them in publishing and design? Firstly, to correctly set a page, to bring a clear focus and to guide the eye to the main content, presenting it in a way that can be best understood and appreciated. Margins are used to stop us from going to the edge, or even off the edge of the page. I always like margins in a book because I can then write in them the thoughts that I suddenly have whilst reading, but if there are no margins, I have nowhere else to write. I have many Bibles, but my all-time favourite is an old, 'wide-margin' New King James one. If you were to look at it, you would see the margins are now filled with comments that I have written over the years as I had revelation concerning verses that I was reading. Margins serve a great purpose in books and they also do in our life! As with books, if you have no margins in your life you have no 'extra space' to use when you need it and you always run the risk of 'leaving the page'.

We have need of all manner of margins in our lives, margins that stop us from 'going over the edge' and enable us to work sustainably. This includes margins in our emotions, energy, time and also our finances.

EMOTIONAL MARGINS

When it comes to your emotions, is there a margin in your life when you need it, or do you continually live on the edge emotionally? If you continually live on the edge, you are actually just waiting to be a victim of the infamous 'straw that breaks the camel's back'. That final thing that will push you over the edge of what is manageable or sustainable for you. I don't believe this is the wisdom of God for someone's life and the emotional layout of the page of our lives should be much better set than that. There should be margin or 'spare area' that, at different times, we can go into when we need to because we don't continually live in it. How many people, even very spiritual people, seemingly all of a sudden breakdown because something relatively small happens that puts

> There should be margin or 'spare area' that, at different times, we can go into when we need to because we don't continually live in it.

a fresh or increased demand on their emotions and it is at that moment they realise they have nowhere else to go emotionally and nothing more to give? So this becomes their breaking point. We were made to live better than this so, if you need to, remove or resolve some things from your emotional page to give yourself (the soul of who you are) somewhere to go when things get emotionally busy or tough. Don't live continually on the edge of what you can emotionally handle, create some margin. I love the picture of the principle of this that we see in Leviticus when it speaks of harvesting fields you have sown.

When you reap the harvest of your land, do not reap to the very edges of your field or gather the gleanings of your harvest. Leave them for the poor and for the foreigner residing among you. I am the LORD your God.
Leviticus 23:22 (NIV)

Basically the Lord was telling them to sow their whole field, but don't harvest it all. Leave a margin! Here, the margin or edge that was left was for the benefit of others, but when it comes to the field of our lives, especially when it comes to our emotional well-being, this edge or margin is most often for our benefit, to keep us healthy so that we can continue to be a blessing to others. You can't give to others what you don't have; make sure the balance of what you have is sustainable by not living continually on the edge of the page.

As I said before, margins can affect a number of different areas in your life and they can have a positive effect on your overall well-being, so it is good to sit and think about their presence in some of the other areas of your life also. I highly recommend sitting down with a friend that you trust and having an honest discussion about them, because sometimes others, from their zero-gravity view of our lives, see what we can't or won't.

FINANCIAL MARGINS

Another major area of our lives where an absence of margins can affect your overall well-being is in our finances. So many people today, especially in the west, live under incredible stress and pressure because of a lack of margin in the financial page of their lives. To put it bluntly, they always have more going out than is coming in, and live constantly trying to justify the deficit in this one issue. I have to be honest and say that when I look back over my life, this was something that was out of balance for far too long, something that brought a continual pressure and limitation on me, my family and things I wanted to do. It can be hard to dream of new things when you're having a problem keeping up with or balancing present things.

Sometimes, having no financial margin is because of things that happened in life that meant that a lack of margin could not be helped or avoided, things like sudden changes in employment or income that could not be controlled. Let's be honest, though, more often than not we were responsible for the out-of-balance problems that have been created in our finances! Some of the 'living on the edge of the page' that we are experiencing financially could have been avoided if we had thought differently. They were the result of common things like wanting things now instead of saving up – 'keeping up with the Joneses' thinking – created from seeing others with things and wanting to have them as well. It can also be the result of other, more practical things like never budgeting or living with an unrealistic budget. Any one of these things could leave us playing catch up or continually paying things off instead of enjoying what we have and being in a position to dream, invest or do new things. Sadly, many people in the western world today are sick, stressed and even having heart attacks because of the pressure that finances are causing in their lives. Let me put that another way, because finances don't cause pressure; how we handle or mishandle them does. Believe me when I say that this pressure has the potential to steal your peace and take your breath away.

> It can be hard to dream of new things when you're having a problem keeping up with or balancing present things.

If you are reading this bit and saying to yourself, 'Yep, that's me, and I am sick of it', my question is: how sick of it are you? Are you sick enough to make some drastic decisions regarding re-budgeting? Once again, let me say that I am specifically speaking to those who can bring some order to their finances not those who maybe can't at this time; if you're someone who can't because maybe things have piled up on you, please seek some advice, don't let them keep piling up. Speak to a debt agency that can help you to make a longer-term plan for your financial freedom.

Back to those who can do things to change the margin of outgoings superseding incoming, I encourage you to not just pray, but do something very practical as well. Get a piece of paper and take a fresh look at your finances and make some brave choices to purposely create some margin in them. This will not just give you space to dream about future things but shift from your shoulders the constant worry and stress of how you are going to make it through the month.

We live in a world where we are constantly bombarded with advertising – everywhere we turn we are being told we need something else. The very premise of advertising is to convince us that we lack something, because if we can be convinced we lack something then we can be sold something else. Come on! It is time for us all to get off the hamster wheel, to re-evaluate what we have and what we actually need so that we can find a place of greater, more genuine contentment. So when it comes to finances make sure there is margin; if there is not then talk to someone who understands handling finances to get any help or advice that you can. As we have said throughout this book, when we come back into Eden through Christ,

God becomes the provider of our lives and gives us everything we need, but that does not mean He gives us everything that we want or think we need! This is where we need to walk with His wisdom. So, concerning the pages of your emotions and finances and any of the other significant pages that make up the book of your life, check your margins are in position and working.

2) HEALTHY COMPARISONS

Another thing we can all experience that has the potential to cause an inner striving that can take our breath away is comparisons. Ever comparing yourself to others? Comparing what you have to what others have, or what you can do to what others can do? This is simply not healthy or good for you, it's a peace-stealer and a breath-taker! It is not wrong to esteem others in a healthy way, to look up to them or be inspired by them – but it is wrong to want to be them. This can create an inner turmoil that is rooted in you actually devaluing yourself. I love the way that Paul speaks about this to the Corinthian church.

We do not dare to classify or compare ourselves with some who commend themselves. When they measure themselves by themselves and compare themselves with themselves, they are not wise. We, however, will not boast beyond proper limits, but will confine our boasting to the sphere of service God himself has assigned to us, a sphere that also includes you . . .

Neither do we go beyond our limits by boasting of work done by others. Our hope is that, as your faith continues to grow, our sphere of activity among you will greatly expand, so that we can preach the gospel in the regions beyond you. For we do not want to boast about work already done in someone else's territory. But, 'Let the one who boasts boast in the Lord.' For it is not the one who commends himself who is approved, but the one whom the Lord commends.
2 Corinthians 10:12-13, 15-18 (NIV)

He starts by simply stating the fact to them, that to measure themselves or compare themselves with themselves, is not wise! Then, he continues on by looking at people simply being true to what God called them to do. As with now, there must have been people in the church then that, instead of just getting on with what they were meant to do, they were watching what others did and wanting to be them or to do what they were doing instead. I love the

> It does not matter what He has asked others to do, what has He asked you to do?

way Paul teaches the error of this by saying God gives everyone their own sphere, a personal circle of responsibility and influence and all He wants them to do is live faithfully within that sphere and not play the game of sphere comparisons. It does not matter what He has asked others to do, what has He asked you to do?

205

Sadly, today within Christian ministry this is an issue that is out of control. So many young ministers in the modern church are striving to be like someone else instead of just being faithful to what God has asked of them, maybe someone they saw at a conference or on YouTube. This becomes a drive within them that causes them not to see or to celebrate what the Lord has given them or made them to uniquely be but, rather, they live in an unrelenting discontent or self-depreciation.

Whether it be in the spiritual or the secular arena of life, purpose not to get pulled into the game of comparisons, rather purpose to 'love the skin you're in'! Celebrate daily who God has made you, what He has given you, and be faithful to what He has asked you to do. One day you will have to give an account for your individual sphere, just as Billy Graham will have to do so for his. In that day I don't want to hear the Lord say to me 'Wow, you just were not happy being you, were you? You were great at impersonating someone else, but at the cost of not being you.' No, I want to hear the words, 'Well done, good and faithful servant, enter into more.'

> Celebrate daily who God has made you, what He has given you, and be faithful to what He has asked you to do.

'His master replied, "Well done, good and faithful servant! You have been faithful with a few things;

I will put you in charge of many things. Come and share your master's happiness!"'
Matthew 25:23 (NIV)

Always remember that it is God who promotes! When we are faithful to the sphere He has appointed us, He then exalts and gives new spheres, so don't you strive to do it or make it happen because striving to be what you're not and to be what someone else is will seriously rob rest from your life. Find a fresh celebration and contentment for your sphere and live faithful to it and, when you do this, you will not experience the breathing issues that others experience because, as Paul put it so well, they are just not being wise!

3) HEALTHY PRIORITIES

Every now and then it's also a healthy thing to take a moment to check your priorities, to make sure they are in correct order. Because, when your priorities are out of alignment to what they should be, it can have breathtaking ramifications on your overall well-being. Sometimes, when you are feeling breathless it can be because the things you are valuing and giving priority to are not the same or are in a different order to the ones that God says you should have. This world we live in is ever screaming at us what it believes is important and what we should be seeking after the most, ever trying to condition us to what we should give our lives to gain. However, when we open the Word of God we see it gives us our true priorities and if we will make them our focus, they will give us a healthy, prospering and sustainable life that leaves a great and lasting legacy after we are gone.

FIRST THINGS FIRST

So what should we prioritise first in our lives? How about things like family, success or security? None of these things are wrong in themselves and God wants to bless and increase these things in our lives, but none of them, or anything else, should be the first thing we seek. Jesus said we should seek first (above and before all) the kingdom of God and His righteousness (the things He considers to be right). Let's look a little closer at what He was teaching.

Therefore do not worry, saying, 'What shall we eat?' or 'What shall we drink?' or 'What shall we wear?' For after all these things the Gentiles seek. For your heavenly Father knows that you need all these things. But seek first the kingdom of God and His righteousness, and all these things shall be added to you.
Matthew 6:31-33 (NKJV)

Jesus says we are not to worry about the things that those who do not know Him worry or stress out about, rather that we are to make His kingdom and righteousness our greatest pursuit, and the thing we seek first and foremost. As we do, He will take responsibility to add to our lives everything else we need. What things? The things that those who do not know God are killing themselves early to try and get. Did you see the key Jesus offers us? Seek His kingdom first and He will give you the things that would be considered by others the true priorities of your life. Again, when it comes to the greatest things in our life Jesus made it really clear what they are when being questioned by a religious leader who was also a lawyer.

> *Then one of them, a lawyer, asked Him a question, testing Him, and saying, 'Teacher, which is the great commandment in the law?' Jesus said to him, "You shall love the LORD your God with all your heart, with all your soul, and with all your mind.' This is the first and great commandment. And the second is like it: 'You shall love your neighbor as yourself.'* **Matthew 22:35-39 (NKJV)**

When it comes to our priorities and the things that should get first place in our life, Jesus teaches here that our greatest priority should be to love God with everything we are and to love others as ourselves, as well as seeking first His kingdom and righteousness. This means that we are uncompromisingly seeking His rule and reign in every area of our life and are committed to living true to what He reveals to be right living. It is when we do this that we can relax, lean back and breathe concerning the other things that matter, but don't matter as much as Him. So, check today that your priorities are in order because if they are not, that could be the thing that is causing an inner striving within you that is bringing about a degree of breathlessness.

4) HEALTHY HABITS (THE THINGS WE DO ON A REGULAR BASIS)

MANAGING TECHNOLOGY AND SOCIAL MEDIA

Let's face it, in today's world, managing technology and social media must now be near the top of the list of managing habits in so many lives. The fact is, what was invented to be a blessing and an assistance to our life can sometimes take a wrong place of time-taking or emotional control in them. Just a generation or so ago, no one could have imagined how things like social media would become so much a part of a person's daily life. I may sound like a bit of an antique to younger readers but I did not own a mobile phone until I was around thirty years old. Prior to that there was no Internet, World Wide Web, emails or social media. People used phones that did not leave home because of the wires connected to them, and we sent letters and postcards to stay in contact with people. I know right, hasn't life moved on so fast?

Now, pretty much everyone has a mobile device or two which gives them the ability to contact people in a whole bunch of ways, and also connects them to the World Wide Web and this thing called social media, from wherever they are whenever they choose.

As with a lot of things available to us in our modern

world with its technology, there are so many great uses for these platforms, including evangelism, discipleship and finding out more about what God is doing in the world today. But, sadly, there are also other things that unknowingly, at the start, have the potential to become highly addictive and time-consuming things in our lives. One of these being what we know as social media. Platforms like Facebook, Instagram and Twitter constantly invite us to 'keep an eye on what the world is doing' and also enable us to 'let the world know what we are up to'. It is amazing when spending time with some people, you soon realise that many have more of a life on social media than they do in actual real day-to-day living and often, without knowing it, are now living their lives vicariously through the lives of others.

Drive down the road as schools and colleges are turning out and you see armies of people walking with heads bent down checking on the well-being of the world, and sometimes so hypnotised by social media life they don't even notice the cars braking or swerving to avoid them. Go out to a restaurant and couples are no longer staring adoringly into each other's eyes, but are checking what's new with their friends and the celebrities they are following. I don't think there is anything wrong with social media and it can be an amazing way of staying in touch with people, especially when they are far away. I use it myself, as do my family, but I do think we need to wise up a bit and use it more soberly, to maintain that it does not take a place in our lives where it becomes an obsession rather than a benefit.

For many people today, their social media has become the first thing they check when they wake up and the last thing they check before going to bed; they check it when travelling, watching a film on the TV and even on the toilet. It is a part of every break in their life and included in every breathing space they may have. My question is simple: how healthy is that for us really?

Once again, for most of us this is simply an issue of margins. If you can't stop or control yourself checking social media, you are probably best unplugging yourself for a while until you can, or even going back to a gadget that does not allow you to, even just for a time, until you get the control back. An obsession to be always checking on your friends and what's happening in their lives really is not healthy and will steal peace and tranquillity from your life. Let's face it, with the way technology is going it is only going to get worse, so put some strong margins in place to stop it becoming a bigger part of your life than it should be. Strong margins that determine things like:

- Where and when you check social media.
- How often you check it and how often you feel you need to check it. A screentime app can be of great assistance with this, but don't be annoyed when it tells you the truth!

Another vitally important question to ask while on this subject is: do these portholes or windows of social media and other media-related things let into your life and home only things that are good for you and things that please God? A good example of this obviously being pornography! Sadly, pornography is no longer 'a magazine on the top shelf of a newsagents'; it's all around us and readily available to us. Far from harmless, pornography will harm your soul and cause contention and damage within you as you try to please God and your flesh in the same being of who you are. This contention of negatively fuelling the flesh of who you are that then causes a battling against the purity of the Spirit within you will take your breath away in a very significant way.

It launches you into guilt, shame and a constant cycle of the need of repentance. Your breathing will become shallow instead of deep and healthy as God intends. We would not let a porn star or a stripper into our living room, would we? But that is what we do when we do not manage what comes through these portholes now positioned in our lives and homes. Sadly, today children watch porn in playgrounds and bedrooms when correct monitoring of their gadgets and their friends' gadgets are not enforced or overseen. As we well know, it is not just an issue for children, is it? Many adults are daily destroying their souls and losing themselves in addictions that can destroy their lives, relationships and their walk with God because of the abundance of pornography available today everywhere you turn. Protect your soul and protect your family by having clear boundaries and margins in place concerning what the Internet and film industry are allowed to bring into your life and home.

Let me underline again, these things can have a very real effect on your quality of breathing, peace and inner sense of wholeness as well as exposing you to the pull and grip of pornography that awakens appetites in you that were not meant to be awoken. As I have heard it said so well: to protect your heart you have to protect the gates into your life. The gates of what you see and what you hear are very real entrance points, so be a watchman at those gates to monitor what is trying to come through them.

> *Finally, brothers and sisters, whatever is true, whatever is noble, whatever is right, whatever is pure, whatever is lovely, whatever is admirable—if anything is excellent or praiseworthy—think about such things.*
> *Philippians 4:8 (NKJV)*

Though it seems strange to some, life was fine for thousands of years before all of these modern gadgets were invented; people did other things with the gift of time they had been given. Make sure you have not exchanged other things like real-life communication with people, reading and thinking, for a plugged-in life of monitoring other people's lives and dramas. Again, all I am saying is: margins, margins, margins! The golden rule being that you make sure you are controlling it and it's not the other way around. Again, if you are not sure what is reality in this area of your life, then ask those who live with you or do life closest to you for their honest opinion concerning your relationship between you and your phone or gadget. Don't be offended if you don't like what you hear; rather do something about it or maybe, if you are concerned, try a social media fast to see what voice or hold social media actually has in your life.

> Though it seems strange to some, life was fine for thousands of years before all of these modern gadgets were invented; people did other things with the gift of time they had been given.

Why is this so important, you may ask? Because you need space to think, meditate and process. God made you this way so that you could resolve, conclude and plan and not blow up or break down. Sometimes it is exactly this that is stolen from us when we cannot spend a moment unplugged from social media or technology. God never made you to live this way; modern society and gadget companies did. If you want to breathe properly in life you need to dare to address this if it is, or could be, an issue, and purpose to do life the way that God designed you to. To have a life that has nothing that has become an obsession, or is setting its pace or state of well-being, is a life where everything has its correct place, including having space or times when we are purposely doing nothing.

This should indeed be an investment that we all make to benefit our overall mental and emotional well-being and to ensure that we are living within the correct rhythms which your life was made to know, and even in a media-driven age still needs. Whether it be social media, gaming, TV or any other additive of modern life, know where the off switch is and when to use it! Govern the time you give to these things rather than letting them govern the time they are going to take from you. See your life (days and hours) as the greatest currency you possess and as a currency that when spent is gone. Purpose not to waste the currency of your life on things that are really not deserving or worthy of them because, if you allow them to, they will take all of your time and not really, in the grand scheme of things, give you much back in return. So, my warning to you is simple: control the activity of these silent time-thieves in your life, give them their margins and use them for what you need them to be, and no more.

> Whether it be social media, gaming, TV or any other additive of modern life, know where the off switch is and when to use it!

> *See then that you walk circumspectly, not as fools but as wise, redeeming the time, because the days are evil.*
> **Ephesians 5:15-16 (NKJV)**

Or as the Amplified Translation puts it in a much 'louder' way:

*Therefore see that you walk carefully [living life
with honor, purpose, and courage; shunning those
who tolerate and enable evil], not as the unwise,
but as wise [sensible, intelligent, discerning people],
making the very most of your time [on earth,
recognizing and taking advantage of each opportunity
and using it with wisdom and diligence], because
the days are [filled with] evil. Therefore do not be
foolish and thoughtless, but understand and firmly
grasp what the will of the Lord is.*
Ephesians 5:15-17 (AMP)

HAVE TIMES OF RE-CREATION

The word 'recreation' comes from the meaning 'to recreate'. Do things that create a sense of well-being in the three-part being of who you are and that cause you to enjoy deep breathing that energises you. Do some things each week that cause you to experience re-creation. Things that specifically enable you to think and to breathe at a better pace. Being that we are all so very different, this is a very bespoke thing; for one person this may be going for a bike ride in the country, for another gardening or fishing. What's the thing that you love doing that causes you to smile on the inside? Do you know? If you don't then find it. If you do, then do more of it! Remember, we are looking at things that bring deeper breathing to the soul and body of who we are, so that what God does in the spirit of who we are is not wasted but complemented. Once again, allow me to say probably to the great annoyance of some: turn off Facebook, Instagram and Netflix and go discover or do something that causes you to experience a deeper sense of fulfilment and contentment.

HEALTHY EATING AND EXERCISE

Without sounding like some kind of fitness guru – which, if you know me, I am certainly not – and being fully aware that we live in a society where everyone seems to keep on about the benefit of these things, we have to recognise that these two specific disciplines really are beneficial to our overall well-being and how we can feel. Yes, they predominantly concern the third of our being called 'our body' but remember, it is a key part of who we are and its well-being can certainly affect how we feel in our soul. The reality is that getting good or balanced nutrition does not just affect your weight, but how you feel as well. Like the old saying goes, 'Garbage in, garbage out.' You cannot expect to experience good well-being in your life, especially long-term well-being if you are eating things that make you feel like sleeping continually. In the same way, exercise does not just benefit your body but your mind as well. Whenever I get a lethargic jam in my life, I head to the gym. There is something about exercising that blows cobwebs out of the brain and gets you thinking sharp and creatively again.

I warned you that this chapter was going to be more holistic than the others, but it is so true that the physical does have a relationship to the spiritual part of who you are, because you are a triune being. I am not going to tell you what to eat, as I am not a nutritionist, or tell you how to exercise because I am not a personal trainer and I have my own struggles. I simply want to say that you should know by now what right eating looks like for you, the things that are good for you and the things that are not, according to how you are wired. These may indeed even include things like gluten or caffeine consumption. You know the amount of exercise that you need to feel good, be committed to making it happen so that your new way of breathing in God's life is not constantly attacked or affected by a lack of natural well-being.

For physical training is of some value, but godliness (spiritual training) is of value in everything and in every way, since it holds promise for the present life and for the life to come.
1 Timothy 4:8 (AMP)

GET YOURSELF OUTSIDE

Without again trying to put all the blame on your smartphone or other technical devices, it is amazing how sitting in a chair, checking social media or watching another streamed box set may seem fun and relaxing. However, it is also sometimes robbing you of going outside and enjoying some fresh air. Forgive me for again sounding ancient but when I was a child we played outside! So much of what we do today involves being inside, with computers, game consoles and televisions.

God did not create you to exist in such environments. In Genesis it does not say: 'In the beginning God made man and placed him in a concrete building with four walls.' No! He made a creation for Adam to enjoy. A world for him to discover, experience and enjoy.

There is just something about being outside that does the soul of you good. Whether it is hearing the waves lap on the shore, smelling freshly-cut grass or watching the leaves change colour in autumn, in the forest. There is something about spending time in the great outdoors that causes a deep, satisfying breathing within us. So, if you don't already, purpose to spend some time each week 'somewhere green'. I know in my life, if I don't get myself out and walk somewhere that is green on a regular basis I get lethargic, agitated and my creativity rapidly diminishes. I am sure I am not alone in this. Whether it be in a park or by the ocean, make time to get outside and breathe deep, go somewhere that you can appreciate God's handiwork. I guarantee, as you do it will cause fresh breathing and a fresh resuscitation within the soul of your life. In the beginning He created a world for you to enjoy, not a living room. It is true that man has severely trashed some of it, but other parts are still perfect: go take another look at it. It's amazing, and as you do: BREATHE DEEP!

CELEBRATING SILENCE

Another key thing we can do to assist the rest of God happening within us is learn to celebrate silence more in our life. We live in such a loud world, filled with so much noise. It's amazing that sometimes we do not even hear the noise because we are so used to it. Sometimes it's a healthy thing to deliberately shut noise off and instead, celebrate silence. A good example of this happened to me just the other day. Having young children in the house, the TV is on a fair bit. Anyone who has kids knows that does not mean the kids are even watching it! You walk into the living room and turn it off, a few minutes later you hear it back on. It is like people today hate silence and have to fill rooms with noise, and it's not just kids who do that. It was only a few days ago that I drove one of my kids to youth group and as soon as we got in the car they leaned over and turned the CD player on and noise filled the car as per usual. I was actually at this time trying to think some things through, so the noise pretty much ruined that. After dropping my daughter off, I was driving home and was feeling quite irritated but could not work out why. Then I worked it out: the CD player was still blaring out music, even though my child was no longer there. Then I had a moment of genius: I leaned over and turned it off! That's right, I turned it off and silence filled the car and peace my soul at the same time. In that now-quiet moment driving home I realised that my soul sometimes loves and yearns for silence and does not want noise, even worship-music noise playing in the car. Not that I am now going to become a monk and swear a pledge of silence, but I have realised that there is room in our western lives to create and celebrate silence a whole lot more than we normally do in our worlds filled with all manner of sound.

Do we sometimes forget that we have the power to turn certain noise off? Do we get so used to an absence of silence that we no longer miss it? Do we forget to sometimes unplug from the noise of this world and get out and about somewhere to enjoy the sound of silence? If so may we remember, because silence is good for us, some of the greatest things the Lord has said to me have come in moments of silence when noise had deliberately been turned off. Maybe He is speaking much more than we have known, but we can't hear Him over the noise of the life we are living in. May I challenge you to consider how you could make room to celebrate silence more because in silence comes great peace and reflection that are good for your soul.

> Do we sometimes forget that we have the power to turn certain noise off? Do we get so used to an absence of silence that we no longer miss it?

And that ye study to be quiet, and to do your own business, and to work with your own hands, as we commanded you.
1 Thessalonians 4:11 (KJV)

5) HEALTHY PACE

Every individual life has a pace of its own when it comes to the speed at which people live. One person's pace can be very different to another's, according to their wiring and personal capacity. The important question we can all ask ourselves is: who is setting your pace? Are you setting it, bearing in mind what is correct for your well-being, or are you knowingly – or worse, unknowingly – letting other people or things set the pace of your life?

Other things can be:

- Other people who think you should or could be doing more.
- A low self-esteem and inner strivings to be better than what you think you are.
- Competitive thinking that drives you to want to be better than others.
- The way you were raised by your parents and others, as they set the example of a 'correct pace' for you in your formative years.
- Things you need to or have to do to make or sustain a living for you and your family.

Any one of these things, and plenty of others, can be the triggers to what sets the pace you are living by, but another question that is important would be: is your current pace, though pleasing to or approved by others, beneficial or sustainable for you and your family? Does it cause you to get the very best out of the life He has blessed you with? If no, what are you able or willing to do about it?

This naturally leads us to the next obvious question which is: can you afford to change your pace if you needed or wanted to? Sometimes, people say they want to change their pace but they can't afford to. Sometimes this is true, other times not so much. As you begin to dig into what they actually do and why they do it, you often find that they are overworking or running at an unsustainable pace in their life, not to sustain their life but to get more things they think they need. Yes, I am talking again about stuff and about 'keeping up with the Joneses'. We must remember that stuff does not define us or determine our true wealth in life, rather other things like our relationship with God and others and our enjoyment of life do.

It is amazing how many times, as a pastor, I hear about couples who got married to be with each other, to have 'more precious time' with each other and for the first few years that is what they do. They live without much 'stuff', and they find the fulfilment they desired in each other. Then the 'stuff' starts building – houses, devices, careers, holidays, cars, etc. – and before long they turn around and they are both working two jobs and not getting any 'precious time' with each other because they have to pay for the extras that are now, apparently, a 'vital part' of their life. This is a common scenario outplayed in many homes in our western world today because we live in a consumer-minded age but that does not make it right or make it healthy for a person or a relationship!

Sometimes it is not until the moment something breaks that people stop and talk about their pace of life and then try to make sudden changes that will cause a last-minute rescue or greater sustainability. That's not godly wisdom, rather the wisdom of the world that says 'you don't know what you have until it's gone'. I believe God's wisdom tells us to know what we have while we still have it and value and enjoy every moment of it! Whether it be a relationship, our health or even our age, do things before there is a problem or a breakdown – do them before you turn around one day and realise that you can't anymore.

Some good questions that only you can answer:

- Do you need to work as hard as you do or as much as you do?
- Are you over-working or striving for things you really don't need, you just want?
- Have you lost a state of contentment for the things you already have?
- Do you need bigger or newer things if your time and healthy life pace is what they cost you?
- Do you need to or can you change your job or hours to accommodate a healthier, more balanced way of living?
- How long can you continue at the pace you currently have?
- When it comes to earning money: when for you is enough actually enough?

These are great questions to honestly ask yourself but they are also great questions to again include other people in, especially your family if you have one. As it was once said so well: 'On a man's deathbed he does not ask to see his business awards or golf trophies.' Make what matters matter now! Again, addressing these things may not affect your spiritual breathing but they will affect the other breathing patterns of your life, and certainly do affect whether or not you live in and from a condition of rest.

6) HEALTHY CONTENTMENT

Living from a place of contentment, or to put it another way 'being content', is of great gain in a person's life and their state of personal well-being, and can cause a very healthy way of breathing throughout the entirety of a person. Similar to healthy comparisons, having healthy contentment is the result of not always looking at what you don't think you have but knowing what you do have, as well as realising, from maybe a more worldwide viewpoint, you more than likely already have all you need to be content. Contentment is the condition of walking in gratefulness and thankfulness instead of greed, comparison and disappointment. It is the fruit and sum total of adding up your life with correct perception and a healthy understanding of what you presently have and how blessed you already are.

The best message I ever heard on contentment came from my wife Gina when she spoke to our leaders at a meeting. It was so good and I was so personally challenged by it. Among other great points that she shared she taught that contentment is something that lives in the deep, inner part of who we are and should never be lost or overly affected by what happens with things that are on the outside of who we are. She taught that true contentment is never lost in changing times or seasons that you may be going through and is not governed by times being prosperous or not so prosperous. She drew our attention to what the Apostle Paul said concerning being content and how his contentment was not affected or determined by times of lack or times of plenty (abasing and abounding) and how firstly he learned to be content and secondly he had found what he called the 'secret of being content' in these different or varying times. The truth is that, like Paul discovered, contentment is something that we can learn if we have a heart to learn and is also a secret that we can find if we are looking.

> *I am not saying this because I am in need, for **I have learned to be content** whatever the circumstances. I know what it is to be in need, and I know what it is to have plenty. **I have learned the secret of being content** in any and every situation, whether well fed or hungry, whether living in plenty or in want. I can do all this through him who gives me strength.*
> *Philippians 4:11-13 (NIV, emphasis mine)*

Paul also demonstrated that true and lasting contentment

227

only comes from being 'in Him' and knowing His life, strength and ability now in you. When you read what Paul went through because he chose to follow and not deny Christ, it paints a picture of a very tough life. If you don't believe me then go take a read about what he claimed happened to him in 2 Corinthians 11. Shipwrecks, whippings, abandonment – the list goes on and on. Yet, despite all these things, he knew a contentment deep within. Why? Because he knew God and he knew the life that comes from God within his own. And so can we! Don't look to things that can never give you contentment to fill your contentment tanks, otherwise you will always feel discontent. No, instead learn contentment in what you go through and find the secret of contentment which is Him. As Paul said to his son in the faith, Timothy, godliness with contentment is great gain and cannot be found in money or things but in our personal pursuit of God!

> *But godliness with contentment is great gain. For we brought nothing into the world, and we can take nothing out of it. But if we have food and clothing, we will be content with that. Those who want to get rich fall into temptation and a trap and into many foolish and harmful desires that plunge people into ruin and destruction. For the love of money is a root of all kinds of evil. Some people, eager for money, have wandered from the faith and pierced themselves with many griefs. But you, man*

of God, flee from all this, and pursue righteousness,
godliness, faith, love, endurance and gentleness.
1 Timothy 6:6-11 (NIV, emphasis mine)

Paul modelled a life that was content despite what was happening around him because his life was rooted in Christ. The only area of his life that he was not content should be the same area that we are to be, and that is in regard to our pursuit or knowing of God more. Paul was conscious that there was so much more of God to know and experience that he made it his goal to keep reaching forwards to that which he had not yet known. As he made his contentment all about knowing the Lord, everything else in his life reached a level of contentment, because they were not as important or valuable as they had once been. When we seek first Him and His kingdom, other things that we think will make us content will find their correct place too. As it was for Paul, so it is for us – true contentment is found in Him alone!

Not that I have already attained, or am already
perfected; but I press on, that I may lay hold of that
for which Christ Jesus has also laid hold of me.
Brethren, I do not count myself to have apprehended;
but one thing I do, forgetting those things which
are behind and reaching forward to those things
which are ahead, I press toward the goal for the
prize of the upward call of God in Christ Jesus.
Philippians 3:12-14 (NKJV)

7) HEALTHY DEVOTIONAL LIFE

And finally we will conclude with what I believe is the most important of them all: having a healthy and vibrant devotional life! This should never be an optional extra for the believer, especially the believer who genuinely desires to breathe life like God intends for them to. Because we have all been made so wonderfully unique, our devotional lives may be very different or bespoke – but they must be in place, celebrated and protected in our lives. It should never be something driven by guilt, routine or obligation, but rather by desire. At the very start of this book we saw that Adam (mankind) was made to walk with God, his primary purpose being to enjoy communion (sharing daily life) with the One who had made him. This was not something he had to do like a non-negotiable appointment – rather it was something that was far more relational, something he loved to do, and from it he received everything he needed to live the life God had blessed him to live.

> The greatest thing that Adam lost is the greatest thing that has been restored for us! The ability to walk with the Lord in the garden of our daily lives!

We have spent significant time considering what Adam lost in his fall or leaving of Eden but I believe the greatest thing that he lost was walking in the garden with the

Lord every day. The simplicity and beauty of speaking to Him and hearing Him speak back, this was his devotional life with God. We have also spent enough time speaking about how Father God has restored for us, through His Son, everything that we lost in Adam. As we think on this one last time at the end of the journey of this book, may we realise that the greatest thing that Adam lost is the greatest thing that has been restored for us! The ability to walk with the Lord in the garden of our daily lives!

It is not a fairy-tale or a religious obligation, but an incredible life-giving invitation. Think about it, the all-powerful and all-loving creator God wants to spend time with you and me each and every day. Not just in ceremonies or meetings that we arrange to be with Him together, but in the random alone moments of our days as well. The One who holds universes and all things in being is intimately interested and wants to be involved in our daily lives! How we all need a fresh and deeper revelation of this simple yet amazing truth! The question then is: do we want to spend time with Him? That this should even be an option or question in our lives blows my mind.

As with Adam, our heavenly Father does not want to spend time with us religiously, because we were not made for religion but for relationship. But I am sure that you have become aware, as I have, that the reality is that wherever or whenever there is an absence of relationship with God there will always be the presence

BREATHE AGAIN
MANAGING THE TRIUNE YOU

of religion about God! History has sadly proved this time and time again. Let us scream it from the rooftops so all can hear we were made for relationship, not religious procedures and ceremonies! Our individual, private devotional lives and times with Him should be so uniquely different and very bespoke to who we are and how He wired us to be.

To one person, the strongest part of their devotional life may be reading the Word, to another intimate times of worship. To one the importance of the presence of many words, another the celebration of silence and waiting. God did not make us in a 'one size fits all' sausage factory; though we are all made in His image and have now been restored to His likeness, we are all so, so different in the outward expressions of who we are, and also the inner soul of who we are.

This was the intention of the God who designed us – not an evolutionary accident! You see, God is truly an unlimited creator who loves to display how awesome He is in everything He designed. Think of one single expression of His creation: butterflies and moths. According to a Google search I did, there are approximately 12-15,000 species of butterflies and 150-250,000 species of moths, with still thousands of moth and butterfly species that have not yet been found.[6] That's just one glimpse of God expressing Himself in something we would call a bug! And when it comes to flowering plants, according

---

6   The Children's Butterfly Site https://www.kidsbutterfly.org/faq/general/2

to *The Guardian*, as of 2010 there are 400,000 types – that is the variety God gave to things that were only to be the environment that held us! It begs the question: though we are all roughly the same kind of shape physically, how different and unique are we all on the inside? This is why, when it comes to our devotional lives, God does not want us impersonating each other or merely reading prayers out of a common prayer book. Rather, He wants for us to give unique expression to who we are, the person He made us to be especially in our devotional life with Him. Do you know that God wants you to release your colour and not try and be like everyone else or someone you saw pray once that looked like they knew what they were doing? He longs to spend authentic time alone with you – you are more than enough for Him.

There are so many devotional books and tools out there today – in fact, I have written some myself, called *Breakfast of Champions*. These are only there to assist you in your devotional life, not to determine or define it!

PULLING AWAY FROM THE CROWD TO BE WITH HIM

Fuelled by desire alone, we should create times of pulling away from the crowd to be with Him. It is in these times that we get to know Him for ourselves as well as receive instruction and empowerment for what lies ahead of us. How often have we just dashed into the busyness of our lives after throwing a token prayer at Him, so that we don't feel guilty? In doing this we just rob ourselves of the fresh life, wisdom and strength He wanted to give us for our day. Here's a thought: if Jesus pulled away from the crowd to spend time with His Father, how could we be arrogant or foolish enough to think we don't need to? Remember again, Jesus was one hundred percent God, as the Son of God, but also as the Son of Man one hundred percent man. The divine nature and human nature existing together in one expression. As the Son of God He was constantly in union with His father yet He modelled for us, as the Son of Man, a daily dependence and celebration of spending devotional time with His Father. Here are a couple of glimpses of these moments:

Now it came to pass in those days that He went out to the mountain to pray, and continued all night in prayer to God.
Luke 6:12 (NKJV)

Now in the morning, having risen a long while before daylight, He went out and departed to a solitary place; and there He prayed.
Mark 1:35 (NKJV)

So He Himself often withdrew into the wilderness and prayed.
Luke 5:16 (NKJV)

This was a way of life for Jesus, as it needs to be for us. He did not rush off to pray when it all got too much for Him; He loved to spend time with the Father and in those times received all He needed to do all the Father asked Him to. Probably the most dramatic example of one of these times being when we see Him go to spend time with the Father the night before His crucifixion. Jesus had spent time in an upper room preparing His disciples for His leaving; Judas had now betrayed Him to the high priests, so the events that would lead to Him going to the cross had now well and truly begun. Jesus was not unaware of what lay ahead because, as it says in Psalms 40:7, He had come 'in the volume of the book' (KJV). This meant He knew everything that was to take place. As the time of His arrest approached it is interesting to see what He did in those last moments. Did He hold one last public meeting? Put on a final crusade for the people before returning to heaven? No. He actually did the complete opposite. He withdrew with some of His disciples to a garden called Gethsemane. Approaching a certain part of this garden that was to be His secret garden with the Father, He had His disciples stop and wait for Him, leaving behind even those who were closest to Him. He entered then into a place where He stood alone in the audience of one, His heavenly Father.

Then they came to a place which was named Gethsemane; and He said to His disciples, 'Sit here

*while I pray.' And He took Peter, James, and John
with Him, and He began to be troubled and
deeply distressed. Then He said to them, 'My soul is
exceedingly sorrowful, even to death. Stay here and
watch.' He went a little farther, and fell on the
ground, and prayed that if it were possible, the
hour might pass from Him. And He said, 'Abba,
Father, all things are possible for You. Take this cup
away from Me; nevertheless, not what I will, but
what You will.' Then He came and found them
sleeping, and said to Peter, 'Simon, are you
sleeping? Could you not watch one hour? Watch
and pray, lest you enter into temptation. The spirit
indeed is willing, but the flesh is weak.' Again He
went away and prayed, and spoke the same words.
And when He returned, He found them asleep
again, for their eyes were heavy; and they did not
know what to answer Him. Then He came the
third time and said to them, 'Are you still sleeping
and resting? It is enough! The hour has come;
behold, the Son of Man is being betrayed into the
hands of sinners. Rise, let us be going. See, My
betrayer is at hand.'*
Mark 14:32-42 (NKJV)

We see Him greatly troubled in the humanity of
who He was as He wrestled with pressing 'go' on the
things that would lie ahead beyond this quiet moment
in the garden. He comes out of this secret place He

had with His Father to find His friends sleeping, After waking them and asking them to pray, He returns back in. This happening a couple of times as He neared the moment of final committal. Then, after praying the prayer that would take Him beyond the point of no return, 'Father not my will be done but Yours', He knelt in the presence of His Father and received all that He needed to go through all that lay ahead of Him. We then see Him leave the garden, no longer weak or scared but ready, strengthened, as the palace guards arrive and He is betrayed with a kiss from one who was a follower and friend. Nothing we will go through in this life will match what Jesus went through over those next few hours, but in the same way He received everything He needed in a secret place with God, so can we! May Jesus be our example regarding having an effective devotional life with Father God.

It's not about the time of day that you do it, or what you do during it compared to what others may do. It's about you taking time to have a secret garden part of your life that belongs to Him. A place you go alone, a place where no man hears the words of your mouth or indeed the cries of your heart. A place where you walk, kneel and lie in the audience of one: your Father in heaven. Nor does it have to be a designated place: some find a room in their home fitting, others prefer to walk in a forest or by the sea. These things are just a matter of personal preference; what matters is you have a secret garden that you leave others behind to be in!

A healthy devotional life will give you the strength you need to live the life He is calling you to. Yes, maybe you could get by without it, but the question is, why would you want to? I pray that these thoughts encourage you to place fresh value on your devotional life with God or if you have never had one, to open the gate to your secret place with Him today. So much about modern Christianity today is public and done for others to see. You can watch social media video after social media video of people doing good for others, and being filmed while they do it. Or of people praying and even fasting while the cameras pan in for a close up. Yet, Jesus taught that the best of these things should be done in a place that no one knows and a way that no one else sees. Though they may be good to watch and make certain people famous on social media, the truth is that they already have had any reward they are going to get for the things they have done. Yet there remains a greater reward according to Jesus for those that have a private unseen place for their giving, fasting and prayer life. He teaches in Matthew 6 that the Father rewards openly the things done in the secret place. I don't know about you but the applause and accreditation of

There remains a greater reward according to Jesus for those that have a private unseen place for their giving, fasting and prayer life.

man for the things I do pales into insignificance in regard to the rewards that God will give.

And when you pray, you shall not be like the hypocrites. For they love to pray standing in the synagogues and on the corners of the streets, that they may be seen by men. Assuredly, I say to you, they have their reward. But you, when you pray, go into your room, and when you have shut your door, pray to your Father who is in the secret place; and your Father who sees in secret will reward you openly.
Matthew 6:5-6 (NKJV)

So I ask you: do you know the address of your secret place? Have you been there lately? I can guarantee one thing because I have known it myself, that you may go in short of breath but when you come out, you will be breathing deeply and correctly again. That is one of the main reasons we need a secret place each day because it keeps our breathing as it is meant to be.

YOUR STRONGHOLD

Another good way of looking at your devotional life is as your stronghold! Most of the time we speak of strongholds it is negative and in regard to something the enemy is doing in a person's life; we refer to him having a stronghold in the person's life which normally means exactly that he has a 'strong hold' on something regarding them that needs to be broken. But the Bible also speaks of a stronghold being a positive thing in a person's life. King David had a stronghold: it was a place that he would go to when he needed to inquire of the Lord and get strategy for a battle he was in or a situation he was facing. Take a look at this account in 2 Samuel, where you see him visit it:

> *When the Philistines heard that David had been anointed king over Israel, they went up in full force to search for him, but David heard about it and went down to the stronghold. Now the Philistines had come and spread out in the Valley of Rephaim; so David inquired of the LORD, 'Shall I go and attack the Philistines? Will you deliver them into my hands?' The LORD answered him, 'Go, for I will surely deliver the Philistines into your hands.'*
> *2 Samuel 5:17-19 (NIV)*

When the Philistine army rose up against David, because he took his God-given position as king, he heard about it and the very first thing he did was go to his stronghold. This was a place that would have been fortified naturally to enable him and his army to breathe and rest during battles. Within it there would have been a secure place that David went into alone with the purpose of inquiring of the Lord and getting His strategy for victory. David would never go into battle presumptuously, just hoping God was with him; rather he would seek God to know if he would win and what he should do to win. In this instance God said yes to him winning and he went out onto the battlefield not arrogant but confident knowing what the Lord had said and confident that the Lord would break out on the battlefield and give him victory, and indeed He did. David actually named the place 'Baal Perazim', meaning God 'broke out like the waters break out'.

The point here is simple: if you want to experience 'Baal Perazim' in your life and the battles you face, then like David the king, you need to have a stronghold that you go to to inquire of the Lord. This greatest presence of this stronghold should be your devotional life, a daily regular place that you go to hear His instruction.

Later on in the chapter in Samuel we see the Philistine enemy rise again against him because in the previous battle he had beaten them, but not annihilated them. I so love what we see David do next: he went back to his stronghold! Again he didn't just presume and say to himself 'let's just do what we did last time', but rather he went back to his stronghold and inquired of the Lord again because he knew that every battle is different and it was not good enough to just presume on what God was going to do. Rather, he would visit the Lord and let Him reveal a different strategy.

Once more the Philistines came up and spread out in the Valley of Rephaim; so David inquired of the
LORD, and he answered, 'Do not go straight up,
but circle around behind them and attack them in

front of the poplar trees. As soon as you hear the sound of marching in the tops of the poplar trees, move quickly, because that will mean the LORD has gone out in front of you to strike the Philistine army.' So David did as the LORD commanded him, and he struck down the Philistines all the way from Gibeon to Gezer.
2 Samuel 5:22-25 (NIV)

As you can see in the above verses God did indeed have a different plan of attack, because He wanted to defeat this enemy in a much more significant way. The Lord was very specific concerning how David was to act on the battlefield, giving him very detailed instructions. This caused David to again walk onto the battlefield with confidence that he would win. He and his army were obedient to what the Lord had said and a mighty victory was given. Notice also that this time the Lord went out before David and struck the enemy so David just had to then walk into the victory God had given him.

This is another very important aspect of having a healthy devotional life. God does not want you to lose your battles or be surprised by the enemy in them. Rather, He wants to give you prophetic confirmations and strategies. Strategies that may not make sense to others or even your own mind but they will be strategies that bring you into complete and perfect victory. Do you want to see God 'break out like the waters break out' in the battles and situations you are facing? Get the doors of your stronghold open again like the doors of your secret place that we spoke of earlier knowing there is only room in it for one and in it you stand in the audience of the One who gives you the victory.

In this chapter we have looked together at some seemingly practical or very natural things in our lives that can seriously affect the way we breathe. It is truly when we dare to look at our lives from this more holistic viewpoint that you can see how important it is to be breathing well in all three parts of who you are: your spirit, your soul and your body. I pray that as we have journeyed together through some seemingly very everyday things that are a part of all of our lives, you found some things that you could start, tweak or give greater importance or focus to.

In writing this last chapter I must confess that I felt as much the leading of the Spirit in what I was writing – even though it was more practical in nature – as I did in the chapters that preceded it. I believe this is because God loves you spirit, soul and body, and wants you to be experiencing His *zoe* life and a breathing deeply in all three parts. His Spirit is indeed now the fountain of new life within you and its waters really do affect the other two thirds of you as well. When the other two thirds of who you are are in a good place I believe that it causes a glorious explosion of well-being both in you and from you. So, breathe deep!

CLOSING THOUGHTS

$\int$o we have arrived at the end of our journey together. I hope that this book has had a positive impact on your life and helped you to get your breath back. We have covered a lot of good ground together over the last nine chapters, looking at why we were made and how we were redeemed back to everything God originally intended for us to know in Christ. We discovered that Eden is not some place far, far away, rather a new way of life for us in the here and now. We considered in depth our new birth and how we were, through being born again, joined again to His divine life. How, like branches, we are now simply to look to the vine for all we need, the vine being Him. We also considered the great rest that He has invited us to know in Hebrews 4 and discovered how we both enter into it and then remain in it. We looked at the promised carefree life that the Lord says we can know and how we are to now function in life to get the very best out of it. We journeyed through what happens when God's breath is present and the life that it always brings, causing dead things to live and barren things to bear fruit. Finally, we looked at how we should now manage our lives in such a way that we don't lose, through a leaky soul, what God is providing through His Spirit.

So now it is time to purpose in your heart to remain in this 'Eden state of being', to think about how the truths we have looked at together have reset your life and how you can protect and build upon this rest. God does not want you to function outside of 'Eden living' any longer, rather that you would experience the things we have looked at bearing fruit from this day on. I am sure that some chapters spoke louder to you than others. Can I encourage you to go back to them at different times and read them again to make sure you have taken out of them all that you could. It's amazing when we hear or read a message for the first time, we only normally retain a part of the information we have heard or read. So, again, let me encourage you to re-read over and over again chapters that spoke to you until they become persuasion and revelation in your life.

Thank you for taking the time to read this book. I pray that it has been a blessing to your life and walk with God indeed and continues to be one.

and breathe!

PRAYER

*I*hope you enjoyed this book and that is has been both a blessing and a challenge to your life and walk with God. Maybe you just got hold of it and are looking through before starting. Long ago, I made the decision never to take for granted that everyone has prayed a prayer to receive Jesus as their Lord, so am including that as the finale to this book. If you have never asked Jesus into your life and would like to do that now, it's so easy. Just pray this simple prayer:

Dear Lord Jesus, thank You for dying on the cross for me. I believe that You gave Your life so that I could have life. When You died on the cross, You died as an innocent man who had done nothing wrong. You were paying for my sins and the debt I could never pay. I believe in You, Jesus, and receive the brand new life and fresh start that the Bible promises that I can have. Thank You for my sins forgiven, for the righteousness that comes to me as a gift from You, for hope and love beyond what I have known and the assurance of eternal life that is now mine. Amen.

Good next moves are to get yourself a Bible that is easy to understand and begin to read. Maybe start in John so you can discover all about Jesus for yourself. Start to pray – prayer is simply talking to God – and, finally, find a church that's alive and get your life planted in it. These simple ingredients will cause your relationship with God to grow.

Why not email me and let me know if you did that so I can rejoice with you? Tell me about your redemption story.

Andy Elmes, response@greatbiglife.co.uk

ABOUT THE AUTHOR

Andy and his wife Gina are the Senior Pastors of **Family Church**, a multi-congregational church located on the South Coast of England. Andy is a visionary leader who has grown the church from twelve people on its first day to now being a significant and influential church in the UK and beyond.

Andy is also the founder of **Synergy Alliance**, a network of like-minded churches and ministries walking shoulder to shoulder, championing the development of healthy, cross-alliance relationships, and of **Great Big Life**, a ministry established to see people equipped and empowered not only to lead effectively in Church but also in every other section and sphere of life too.

Andy has a wealth of experience and wisdom to offer that comes from a very successful time in ministry. As well as planting churches, he has been involved in many forms of evangelism including travelling as an evangelist for many years across the UK and throughout the world.

A dynamic visionary, Andy helps people to see things outside of the box and, as a strategist, he helps others to set goals within their lives and ministries and move towards them quickly. His experience, combined with his life-coaching skills, makes him a valuable asset to any pastor or leader seeking personal development encouragement and to address change.

A highly sought-after conference speaker for events and conferences, Andy regularly shares on a whole range of subjects including leadership, motivation and evangelism. Andy's versatility allows him to communicate as a pastor, an evangelist, a teacher or coach reaching individuals of all ages and in a variety of settings. Andy is very natural and irreligious in his approach, using humour well and being very animated and often unconventional in his delivery. His desire is to lead people to Jesus and help them to discover all that is now available to them through what Jesus has done for them. His personal mandate is 'to know the King and to advance His kingdom.'

Originally from Portsmouth, this is where Andy and Gina, along with their five children, Olivia, Ethan, Gabrielle, Sophie and Christina, now reside and lead the different ministries from.

USEFUL LINKS

Family Church: **family.church**

Great Big Life: **greatbiglife.co.uk**

Breakfast of Champions devotional sign-up:
breakfastofchampions.co.uk

Synergy Alliance: **synergy-alliance.org**

Synergy Christian Churches:
synergychristianchurches.com

iamredemption: **iamredemption.org**

Talking Church: **facebook.com/groups/
talkingchurch**

ANDY'S SOCIAL MEDIA LINKS
Facebook: **facebook.com/AandGElmes**

Facebook: **facebook.com/
breakfastofchampionsemail**

Twitter: **@andyelmes**

Instagram: **@andyelmes**

ALSO BY ANDY ELMES

Breakfast of Champions, Volume 1
ISBN: 978-09928027-0-7

Breakfast of Champions, Volume 2
ISBN: 978-09932693-2-5

God's Blueprint for His Church
ISBN: 978-09928027-2-1

The Glass of Water
ISBN: 978-14823513-1-6

iamredemption
ISBN: 978-09928027-4-5

Available from **greatbiglifepublishing.com**

FURTHER INFORMATION

For further information about the author of this book, or to order more copies, please contact:

Great Big Life Publishing
Empower Centre
83-87 Kingston Road
Portsmouth
Hants
PO2 7DX
UK

info@greatbiglifepublishing.com
www.greatbiglifepublishing.com
@GBLPublishing

ARE YOU AN AUTHOR?

*D*o you have a Word from God on your heart that you're looking to get published to a wider audience? We're looking for manuscripts that identify with our own vision of bringing life-giving and relevant messages to the Body of Christ. Send yours for review towards possible publication to:

Great Big Life Publishing
Empower Centre
83-87 Kingston Road
Portsmouth
Hants
PO2 7DX
UK

or, email us at info@greatbiglifepublishing.com